THE
ROAD MOST
TRAVELED

13 Common Mistakes for Making Life Miserable

THE
ROAD MOST
TRAVELED

13 Common Mistakes for Making Life Miserable

By Zane Parker Nelson, Ph.D.

CFI
Springville, Utah

ISBN 13: 978-1-55517-948-7
ISBN 10: 1-55517-948-7

Published by CFI, an imprint of Cedar Fort, Inc., 2373 W. 700 S., Springville, UT, 84663
Distributed by Cedar Fort, Inc., www.cedarfort.com

LIBRARY OF CONGRESS CATALOGING-IN-PUBLICATION DATA

Nelson, Zane.
The Road Most Traveled / by Zane Parker Nelson.
    p. cm.
Includes bibliographical references.
ISBN 1-55517-948-7 (alk. paper)
1. Christian life—Mormon authors. I. Title. II. Title: The road most traveled.

BX8656.N45 2006
248.4'89332—dc22

2006014950

Cover design by Nicole Williams
Cover design © 2006 by Lyle Mortimer
Printed in the United States of America

10 9 8 7 6 5 4 3 2 1

Printed on acid-free paper

TABLE OF CONTENTS

Acknowledgments

THE SUCCESSFUL PRESENTATION OF A book can never be the result of one person's efforts. I wish to thank all of the patients and clients I have had over the years for helping me learn the principles presented in this book.

I also wish to express my gratitude to Tracey Smithee who organized this material and provided the golden thread to weave the manuscript into what it has become.

INTRODUCTION

MAX CAME INTO MY OFFICE with a specific request. "Tell me how to mess up my life, Dr. Nelson. I'm experiencing far too much joy. What can I do to ensure that I'll have a life full of misery? Also, how can I mess up my kids' lives? How can I make sure they will never learn responsibility, never honor any values, never become educated, always cause problems for others, and continue to sponge off me forever?"

"Well," I said, "I have a list here of *13 Common Ways To Make Our Lives Miserable.* What's great about these ideas is that they destroy the joy of your loved ones about as much as your own!"

"Great! That's for me!" replied Max as he left my office clutching the list of *13 Common Ways.*

Of course, I've never had anyone come in complaining about too much joy! Nor have I ever had any parent come in asking, "How can I mess up my kids' lives?" Rational people simply do not intentionally seek misery and despair.

Nevertheless, I continue to have numerous patients who come in with incredibly messed up lives or who are struggling to cope with loved ones who have messed up lives.

The big question then is this: If no one actually sets out to intentionally create unhappiness and despair, why is there so much of it out there, even among God-fearing, faith-professing Christians?

More specifically, if Christ has overcome the world through the Atonement, shouldn't Christians, especially members of The Church of Jesus Christ of Latter-day Saints, be the happiest and most joy- and peace-filled people on the face of the earth? (See Mosiah 4:3.) Why then, do so many Christians feel frustrated, angry, sad, depressed, hopeless, discouraged, overwhelmed, inadequate, and often times so completely unhappy?

For more than twenty-five years, I have counseled people with these feelings. Although all people, Christian and non-Christian, have the same basic needs and desires, a number of things specific to Latter-day Saints should prevent this all-too-frequent dilemma and plea for help.

The quest for peace of mind, or mental health, is universal. No one has been given all the internal qualities and the external circumstances that ensure peace of mind. We must work to achieve it. We must strive for a better understanding of ourselves, and then use that understanding to build and maintain more satisfying relationships.

Many of the truths of the gospel have been "rediscovered" by modern psychology. I have found that the principles of the gospel and the principles of good mental health are mutually reinforcing. This book is an attempt to put these principles into layman's language and, in so doing, help us enlarge our understanding of how to keep life in balance, improve our own mental health, help others in their struggles, and increase the ratio of joy to pain that we experience as we "endure to the end" (3 Nephi 27:6).

While disguised as an outline of thirteen ways to make our lives miserable, this book actually represents my sincere desire to help facilitate true and lasting joy. Each of the destructive "mistakes" explored here are rooted in priceless truths. These truths are explored in their own separate chapters, which contain true gospel and mental health principles, open discussion, quotes, and scriptural references. After each thinking error is presented, you will find ways to get out and stay out of these common traps. These truths, principles, and suggestions may, if learned and consistently applied, give the reader, the seeker, the believer, and even the skeptic the inner peace and happiness that we are promised through the good news of Jesus Christ.

Christians often find themselves asking, "What does He want me to do? What does He want me to become?" As difficult as it is to attempt to put ourselves in God's mind, people struggle as well with the origin of grace. We comprehend that love is a conscious decision, but we sometimes cannot understand that God's grace and God's love are His gifts to us.

In the wonderful book *The Road Less Traveled*, Scott Peck tells us that "to explain the miracles of grace and evolution we hypothesize the existence of a God who wants us to grow—a God who loves us. To many this hypothesis seems too simple, too easy; too much like fantasy; childlike and naïve. But what else do we have?" He further states, "Where does love come from? We cannot answer these questions in the same scientific way we can answer where flour or steel or maggots come from. It is not simply that they are too intangible, but more that they are too basic for our 'science' as it currently exists. For these are not the only basic questions that science cannot answer. Do we really know what electricity is, for instance? Or where energy comes from in the first place? Or the universe? Perhaps someday our science of answers will catch up with the most basic questions. Until then, if ever, we can only speculate, theorize, postulate, and hypothesize" (269).

Dr. Peck further introduces us to a loving God who wants us to grow and become like Him. This notion is terrifying to most of us. We simply don't want to work that hard. Millions of people literally run away from this notion in sheer panic.

So, what do you think? Can we become like God? Is our LDS notion of becoming gods and goddesses just grandiose thinking, or is it the reason we are here in the first place? Since mental health is a nebulous subject at best, do we dare hope that we can possibly overcome the "natural man" and develop communication skills, problem-solving skills, personal boundaries, and other essentials that will start us on that path to godhood? I believe we are here for more than mere survival. By the end of this book, I hope to have answered these questions to your satisfaction and perhaps provided reasons for you, too, to believe.

The examples contained herein are for discussion only, and all names and details have been changed and carefully protected. These examples reflect many common situations and feelings that the majority of us have had or will have in this journey we call earth life. Perhaps you will see yourself or someone close to you in these stories. I hope the ideas in this book will spark in you the ability to achieve personal peace and happiness.

Chapter One

NEVER
EXAMINE
YOURSELF

SINCE LIFE IS NOT SIMPLY a bed of nails and this book is not simply about pain management, it is important to remember that life can be full of beautiful and rewarding moments that are explicit in the scriptural statement, "Men are that they might have joy" (2 Nephi 2:25).

A central message throughout this book is that joy can be achieved. Joy doesn't just happen; it develops through a combination of effort and understanding. It is a process.

Similarly, mental health is a process, not a destination or a status. The scriptures instruct us to do this "line upon line, precept upon precept, here a little and there a little" (2 Nephi 28:30; see also Isaiah 28:9–10).

Joy and mental health don't come all at once. People don't ever get to a point where they can say, "I am now mentally well. I am perfect in my understanding of mental health. I have it all together and shouldn't have any more problems from here on out."

I like to think that most of the people who come to see me are in a kind of mental health course. It's a little bit like dieting, learning the stock market, or obtaining a college degree—there are required facts to learn, variables to be considered, and certain demands that put each of us on a unique trek or path of learning.

Having said that, I want to make it clear that I'm not trying to drum up business for all the psychologists in the country. A percentage of the population might never have, and never will, need the benefits of a competent counselor, psychologist, or psychiatrist. In my younger days, I certainly felt I was in that category. During my post-doctoral fellowship, I was required to go to group therapy and have my own personal therapist for one year. In the beginning, I was against it and felt it was a large waste of time. Looking back on it, I now know that it was some of the most beneficial learning time of my entire life.

The unexamined life is not worth living.[1]

Many of us have learned from sad experience that it is often easier to see the faults and shortcomings of others, such as our children, spouses, relatives, and coworkers, than it is to see them in ourselves. It's a case of "the mote and the beam" found in the New Testament in Luke 6:41–42. However, each one of us can learn to examine ourselves with accuracy, maturity, and balance instead of perfectionism, derogation, and ridicule.

It's a process, to be sure. Each day of our lives is a study of humanity and introspection. Ask yourself this question, "Did I handle life, people, and problems better today than I did last week? If not, am I simply along for the ride?" We'll all have days when things get out of hand but, in general, we should be striving toward forward motion or progress.

If I did not have faith that people could change, I could not tolerate being a psychologist. It bothers me deeply to read books on psychology that describe mental ailments but offer no hope for the sufferers. These authors simply approach the problems with stereotypes and tell the reader to resign himself to his fate.

My theory is different. I believe we each came here with trials, challenges, and weaknesses to overcome. The Lord has told us:

> *And if men come unto me I will show unto them their weakness. I give unto men weakness that they may be humble; and my grace is sufficient for all men that humble themselves before me; for if they humble themselves before me, and have faith in me, then will I make weak things become strong unto them. (Ether 12:27)*

There is a reason that the term is *self-examination*. If the term were *spousal-examination* or even *parental-examination*, there would be a whole different set of rules. Have you ever noticed that "I told you so" is the best way to lose friends and alienate people? We each grow at our own pace. When I may be ready to work on self-esteem issues, you may already be on self-mastery. Therefore, we can accept that something that is teaching me great things may not mean anything to you and vice-versa. See if this rings a bell:

"I don't need that," thought Gary in mild irritation. "I take good care of my wife and family. I think I've got my life pretty well in hand." His wife, Donna, was commenting with obvious satisfaction on the wonderful things she was learning about herself from a book she was reading. Gary knew she was talking not only to herself but also to him, hoping he would get interested and read the book also. "That's okay for her," he thought. "Women like that kind of stuff. But we're doing okay. I don't need things like that, and anyway, it would probably bore me."

Donna sighed to herself; "We really *are* doing okay—as a couple, as a family, and as individuals. But there's so much more! I know he'd enjoy the self-reflection once he started reading some of this." Still, having no wish to push, she said very little about it, and in her personal prayers that evening she sincerely thanked Heavenly Father for the good husband she had.

Years later, when Gary was going through a particularly trying time, he found himself becoming more immersed in the scriptures than he had ever been. Additionally, after a colleague of his raved about a certain book, he read it and discovered amazing new tools for putting true gospel principles into practice in his life.

"Honey," he told Donna enthusiastically, "this book is really fantastic. You should read it."

Donna looked at the book. "Yes, it is good, isn't it?" she said, smiling to herself as she realized that this was the book she had recommended to her husband seven years earlier. She said no more about it, however, allowing him to be at a different place, pace, and time than she was.

The story is told about a traveler who stopped by an old farmhouse one day. The farmer invited the traveler up onto the porch to sit a while. As they began to visit, the traveler noted an old hound dog lying a few feet away, snoozing in the afternoon sun. Every few minutes the dog would lift his head and let out the most mournful yowl.

After the dog repeated this several times, the traveler said, "What seems to be the problem with your dog?" The farmer remarked without seeming concerned, "Oh, he's lying on a nail that has popped up on the porch there." The traveler remarked, "Why doesn't he move?" The farmer shared great wisdom as he answered, "Oh, it doesn't bother him enough to move . . . just bothers him enough to complain really loud."

How many of us are in a similar circumstance? How far out of control do our lives have to be before we are bothered enough to change? Do we have to wait until we've had a heart attack to change our lifestyles and eating habits? Do we have to wait until our marriages have fallen apart and our children are getting into trouble in school before we take steps to keep the love alive in our marriages and give our children a foundation of security and responsibility on which to build?

In *The Seven Habits of Highly Effective People*, Stephen Covey talks about how we put out fires in our lives. Instead of being able to prioritize our actions, behaviors, plans, and goals, we run around like amateur firemen, putting out one fire after another or running from one crisis situation to another.

What if we could take some time on a consistent basis to evaluate ourselves? This approach presents an enormous challenge, especially for Christians. Why? Because the New Testament measuring stick—perfection—seems so daunting, even damning.

In the Bible, Matthew instructs us, "Be ye therefore perfect, even as your Father which is in Heaven is perfect" (Matthew 5:48). The Greek text of this scripture uses a different word than perfect. Changing out this word, it says, "Be ye therefore téleios, even as your Father which is in Heaven is téleios." What in the world is *téleios*? Simply put, téleios means complete, balanced, and mature.

Now change the scripture to read, "Be ye therefore complete, balanced, and mature, even as your Father which is in Heaven is complete, balanced, and mature."

Wow! The light came on in my mind and heart when I first heard that! There's hope in téleios; there is possible success! Most of us have figured out that we won't reach perfection during this lifetime. Of course, our Heavenly Father does hope for us to eventually become like Him, but He realizes that it's a process, a journey, a quest.

Some say we have to come close to death, or at least comprehend death, before we can truly learn to live. When I reflect on our lives with the losses, confusions, and pains we all experience, I understand why we often cry as we pass through this mortal life that is sometimes called a "veil of tears."[2]

Often the command to endure to the end can seem overwhelming. My hope is that this book will help you walk your walk and endure to the end. After all, "It ain't over till it's over!"[3]

This story about NFL quarterback Steve Young illustrates this point:

> *Several months after winning the Super Bowl, Young was speaking to a small group of U.S. Marines. One of them asked, "How does it feel to win the Super Bowl?" "Great!" he replied. "It feels great. But you know, after all the wonderful celebration and excitement—and it was very exciting—I found myself thinking one morning, 'What now? Is that all there is? What was it all for?' And I came to a realization that the worth of it all was in the process, not the event." He went on to explain the exhilaration of the effort, the growth, the overcoming of huge obstacles. "I needed to have something to work against in order to grow. I needed the Dallas Cowboys for that.*[4]

On another occasion, Young reportedly concluded a motivating speech by imploring the audience with, "I plead with you to make a study of YOU!"[5]

So, if self-examination is important, where do we start? We're told in the scriptures that "the glory of God is intelligence, or, in other words, light and truth" (D&C 93:36). This means that if we gain more understanding into any aspect of life, we actually become more godlike. What greater challenge could we possibly have than to understand ourselves more fully and to bring ourselves into balance with others and with our world?

The scriptures teach, "And ye shall know the truth, and the truth shall make you free" (John 8:32). While the truth will make us free (unchained, open to learn and grow), the truth may also bother us, at least at first. The truth may hurt, anger, frustrate, confuse, or even frighten us. In fact, we may not really want the truth at all. Many of us, through a myriad of mechanisms, ardently avoid seeing the truth, perhaps even as we think we are seeking it. Nevertheless, if we do not maintain that quest for truth, we will only be marking time. Life will progress beyond us, and even if we started out strong, we will be left far behind. These words were seen on a banner at a business conference:

> *If you want to change your life . . . you're going to have to change your life!*

Maybe this is easier said than done, but establishing a relationship with yourself is the first job to accomplish. When you know who you are and what you want, you may find that your other relationships fall into place. It is best to be familiar with your core self and be actively engaged in nurturing it in directions you want to go in your life. When we uncover this core and accept it and work on it, a more calm, stable, and secure self emerges, full of confidence and self-acceptance. Life then has purpose and happiness; depression and hopelessness are not as evident.

When a child is hurting, parents often turn their attention to the symptom, trying to find where it is, how it feels, and how long it has been there. One of the biggest mistakes in self-examination is to confuse your symptoms with the source of your problems. An example of this would be physical ailments such as headaches, stomachaches, nausea, agitation, irritability, and depression. Can these symptoms be caused by more than one source? Absolutely! For instance, is it:

- Head trauma or food-allergy headache?
- Appendicitis or ulcer?
- Influenza or morning sickness?
- General irritability or sleep deprivation?
- Depression or medication reaction?
- Attention-seeking or true suicidal ideation?
- Common cold or hay fever?
- Diarrhea from irritable bowel, nervous stomach, or food poisoning?

Although these are vastly different causes of pain, they present themselves with similar symptoms.

My patients often hear me say, "Observation is easy; interpretation is difficult."

Many of the physical symptoms that present themselves may actually be our bodies' reactions to financial stress, substance abuse, marital difficulties, troubles raising children, poor diet, post-traumatic stress, or abuse. The reactions of the physical body to emotional stress and trauma are well documented. Again, candid self-examination is crucial.

What causes the flu, measles, or chicken pox? They are not simply viruses. Rather, they are caused by exposure to a virus and the body's inability to resist the virus. Similarly, mental and emotional pain are the result of both exposure to life's problems and our inability or limited ability to cope effectively with those problems. We are not all the same, but we will all be exposed to illness, fatigue, death, lack of respect, differences of opinion, taunting, thoughtlessness, financial stress, employment challenges, unfairness, and disappointment. Differences in upbringing, heredity, experiences, energy levels, personal preferences, and individual capabilities all contribute to making us different. Since we are so different, it only makes sense that our reactions will be different as well.

Many people use their upbringing, their heredity, and their environment to make excuses for the way they behave or react to what goes on around them. In a sense they say, "You can't expect me to dance . . . I have a wooden leg!" These people resist getting emotionally well because of their "wooden leg." Their wooden leg might be uneducated parents, an abusive childhood, poverty, or discrimination, which they fold up into a tidy package of excuses. Anger, frustration, depression, or mental illness can become wooden legs: "You can't expect me to happy and productive . . . I come from such an abusive background" or "You can't expect me not to be angry . . . I've endured such discrimination."

Most of the time we can find people who would commiserate with us because of the trials we have endured and the misfortune we've suffered. Failure is something that everybody can relate to. But, what if we give away our wooden legs and choose to step to a higher level?

Believe it or not, some people are more afraid of success than they are of failure. Failure and disappointment are universal experiences, but success means responsibility, example, leadership—even a form or autonomy. If we never gain knowledge of ourselves, we never have to change our behaviors. If we never change our behaviors, we have a perfect excuse to fail. If we fail, we have our wooden legs to explain to ourselves and all of society why we failed.

I am not implying that wooden legs, or life's challenges, aren't accompanied by real pain. They are. As with many illnesses in the body, however, the pain is not manifested at its source.

THE SISYPHUS COMPLEX

Sisyphus was a mortal man in Greek mythology. He was sentenced by Zeus to roll a big rock up to the top of a hill over and over again for all eternity. If we consider him damned—damned meaning halted or stopped progress—we find that this defines Sisyphus' punishment accurately. Every time Sisyphus succeeded in pushing the rock to the top of the hill, it would, by its own weight, roll back down the hill and into the valley. Because he could not identify a solution to stop the rock from rolling back down the hill, Sisyphus was thus doomed to continually repeat the action forever.[6]

Sisyphus complexes are situations in which people who claim to want to be successful are afraid to be successful. They might say, "I want to lose weight." "I want to graduate from school and make a good living." "I just want to get out of prison and be free." "I want to be active in my church."

The question is, do we really want that? Often we may want the success but we may not want the responsibilities. The futility of Sisyphus' task represents the fears each of us may have of actually getting our rock not only up to the top of the hill but getting it to stay there. Predictably, people do not like being confronted with the possibility that they sabotage their own goals or that they may have a will to fail. My job is to help people realize these fears, face them, and deal with them.

A single mother in her mid-thirties, Sue had several children at home. She had had a weight problem even before her divorce, but since the divorce, she had reached 350 pounds. While she said that one of the main reasons for seeking help was to lose weight, we soon realized that her weight had become her wooden leg. She eventually admitted that because of her religious background, the most terrifying thing she could imagine—even more terrifying than death—was being sexually involved outside of marriage. In time, she realized that her weight was her insulation from men and from sexual contact. She reasoned, "Who would be attracted to a three-hundred-fifty-pound woman?"

We worked on her self-confidence. Eventually, she realized that women can be thin and virtuous.

With this knowledge, she gave up her wooden leg, began losing weight, started socializing, and became much more outgoing and happy.

I want to make two points regarding causal factors, which very simply are factors that cause or produce other things. First, biological problems are an important causal factor in many common classes of emotional disorders, including depression. Any attempt to change the way any individual thinks or acts must include an understanding of potential biological factors. For instance, regardless of how much experience a famous collegiate track coach may have, how encouraging he is, or how successful he has been in the past, he will never be able to teach a severely anemic person to run a mile race well unless first he first treats the anemia. In like manner, no matter how competent the counselor, a person will never do well if a physical problem affects thought, mood, attitude, energy, or general reasoning.

The second fundamental causal factor is feelings. When I stress the importance of good feelings, I am referring to what I call core feelings. These involve emotions that cannot be reached through chatting about the weather, though I often discuss irrelevancies as icebreakers to initiate discussions about sensitive or painful matters.

Put simply, if good feelings and proper biological functioning are present in a person, good symptoms are usually evident. Conversely, if negative feelings are present or a biological breakdown is impairing emotional health, negative symptoms are presented.

Not every mental illness has a physiological basis, but some clearly do. Unfortunately, it is not uncommon in our culture to encounter resistance to help and especially refusal to take medication that is clearly needed. Some people may fear negative side effects or addiction. They may conclude that our society's abuse and overuse of medications means that all medicines are bad. Some people with extremely serious disorders falsely believe that if they just trust enough in the Lord, they won't need medication. Many people feel an unfortunate negative stigma is associated, even today, with the use of mental health medications.

The truth is that most of these medications do not create physical addictions or psychological dependencies. Instead, they replenish deficient chemicals in the body, just as insulin does for a diabetic. Thankfully, we are nearly to the point where there will be no greater stigma attached to chemical imbalances that cause psychological and emotional problems than to imbalances that cause diabetes or thyroid malfunction. Furthermore, evidence clearly shows that wise use of medication has helped many people turn their lives around. Many people have felt led by the Spirit to particular doctors who have been able to diagnose and prescribe medication.

Certainly psychological counseling is needed with any prescribed medicines. If a physical problem exists, the whole improvement process can be greatly accelerated with medication and therapy. Medical knowledge and technology have made tremendous strides over the years in diagnosing and treating mental health illness. It would be a terrible shame to ignore this progress and stoically refuse the help that is available to curtail the suffering.

Now that we've evaluated ourselves, learned who we truly are, found the help of a qualified mental health professional, and identified the question of whether medication is necessary or appropriate, let's get on with it! It's time to get well!

Chapter Two

BELIEVE IN QUICK FIXES

BY THE TIME A REASONABLY healthy, and sufficiently educated person has had a few visits with a competent mental health professional, he is, for all intents and purposes healed! Right?

Wrong! One of the most self-defeating things we do is establish deadlines, labels, and boundaries for getting well. We refuse to believe that some illnesses are life-long. However, while some depression, anxiety, and other mental health issues are situational (your husband loses his job, your best friend dies in an accident, you need to recuperate after major surgery), others become chronic, recurring, cyclic, and chemically based in the brain. It is as ridiculous for a person with a chemical imbalance to stop taking medication and receiving counseling as it would be for a person with high blood pressure to decide that he has been on medication long enough and he just won't have high blood pressure any more. The body doesn't work that way!

The mind is an amazing thing. Sometimes, individuals who are depressed actually experience secondary gains. We don't consciously choose depression; however, at times we actually have subconscious reasons for getting depressed. Unfortunately, regardless of the reasoning, depression can eventually lead to biological breakdowns.

Hidden reasons for depression may include the following:

- **Avoiding responsibility:** We don't expect children or young people to shoulder a lot of responsibility. If we are depressed, we can return to a younger state in which we don't have responsibility. Someone with depression might say, "You can't expect a depressed person like me to function like a responsible adult!"
- **Attention-seeking:** Wanting sympathy, wanting the attention of people.
- **Self-fulfilling prophecy:** "I know that something bad is going to happen." Therefore, it is like a preemptive strike. Be ready for the depression. "I'm already here, so when it hits it doesn't hurt so bad." It's rather like an insurance policy with paid-up insurance or a medical savings plan.
- **Expiation of guilt:** Like joining the cult of flagellants (people who cut, flog, whip, or crucify themselves), these people beat themselves into a "woe is me—look how bad I've been" way to gain attention from God, to get God's forgiveness, or even to identify with Christ.
- **Identification with a martyr:** Christ cried out, "My God, My God, why hast thou forsaken me?" (Mark 15:34). He had previously pled, "Father, if thou be willing, remove this cup from me" (Luke 22:42). Many people do not see the happiness in Christ. They see the depression part, the sadness that He must have felt as He atoned for the sins of the world.

There is a difference between sadness and depression. When feeling down, it's good to know which is which! But remember:

There is no pill for sadness.

Life is full of trials and challenges; that's part of why we're here. We've all heard the comparisons: You have to know the bitter to appreciate the sweet; you have to see the clouds to appreciate the sun.

> *For it must needs be, that there is an opposition in all things. If not so . . . righteousness could not be brought to pass, neither wickedness, neither holiness nor misery, neither good nor bad.* (2 Nephi 2:11)

The truth is that there are no quick fixes in life. If you've ever watched a chick trying to hatch out of its shell, the sight is tedious, even bloody and gruesome. The struggle, pecking, and butting are tremendous. A caring person may instinctively break the egg and facilitate the chick's exit. However, such action actually makes the chick weak, so weak it might not survive. The struggle to break free actually makes the baby chick strong enough to survive!

In the well-known hymn "Come, Come Ye Saints," we hear the words, "And should we die before our journey's through, Happy day! All is well!" Simplistically speaking, the pioneers experienced the most difficult of circumstances. They fought cold, heat, starvation, illness, death, and suffering. We gain perspective when we think about the hardships they went through, and yet they demonstrated incredible attitudes of faith and solace and believed that "all is well!"

As Christians, we instinctively know that all is well; that is what our faith teaches us. If we feel we could face death with an "all is well" attitude, why are other crises so overwhelming to us? Why are back taxes, poor grades, high grocery bills, unemployment, marriage harmony, and raising kids such a trial? Why do we talk the talk of faith but sometimes walk the walk of cowardice?

Crises, pressure, and trials are often a matter of mindset, attitude, and faith. Therefore, as we look at opposition in all things, realizing that there are lessons to be learned, challenges to be overcome, examples to be set, and joy to be obtained, we find that we can grow from numerous things, both good and bad. Our spirits wouldn't integrate and become whole or complete without all of these experiences. More than the experiences themselves, however, it is actually *our* definition of those things that is crucial.

We often talk in extremes. We say, "It was horrible" when talking about being caught in traffic. We say, "I nearly died" when talking about an embarrassing moment. We say, "I can't stand it" when referencing our annoyance to a puppy whining outside. Our personal viewpoints can make our circumstances much worse than they actually are. It takes great discipline and self-determination to avoid using extremes when talking about everyday events.

How was that traffic jam really? It might have been tedious. It might have been boring. But was it horrible? And, what about that embarrassing moment? Imagine you're a young man going into choir class one day with the zipper on your pants unzipped. A friend leans over and says, "Hey, check your zipper!" Certainly, that could be surprising or a little embarrassing, but did you truly nearly die?

And let's say that you have a new puppy—and several young children. A child or a puppy seems to be making noise all the time. You've had a long day and your nerves are on edge. The puppy has been whining for nearly fifteen minutes. Of course you're tired of listening to the noise. You're probably tense and a little frustrated, but can you stand it? Is there anything about that little bit of noise that could actually lead you to pass out, lose consciousness, have a seizure, or die? Of course not!

Sometimes referred to as making a mountain out of a mole hill, many of us become trapped by common exaggerated phrases like these. You see, life is a process of self-mastery and growth. Not only is our perspective on what is going on around us important, but our self-talk, attitudes, and perspectives will color, flavor, and affect every part of our path.

One of my foster fathers, Lyle R. Peterson, was a man of tremendous influence who taught me well. Among his teachings to me was the following poem that helped me to understand that it wasn't what I became but who I became that mattered:

SELF-MASTERY
What though I conquer my enemies and lay up store and pelf,
I am a conqueror poor indeed until I subdue myself.
What though I read and learn whole books while I am young, I am a
linguist in disgrace who cannot guard my tongue.
What though on campus I excel, a champ in meet and fight,
If trained deficient still I can't control an appetite.
What though elections write my name high on the Honor Roll,
Electives, solids fail me if I learn no self-control.
And what though I graduate and soar and life is good to me,
My heart shall write me failure until I learn self-mastery.[7]

Of course our education, upbringing, religious beliefs, and overall health can affect our perspective in a given situation. Let me share a personal story:

A few years ago my son, Scott, who was 34 years of age, was murdered in Cambodia, where he was a director of a security agency. The law in

Cambodia states that the body has to be cremated within 24 hours. We chose not to follow that. It is our tradition to have regular burial, and we needed a body for our personal closure. However, it took us twelve days to get the body back to the United States. During those twelve days, I continued some of my work, and after that, I continued working. Another doctor in the building would see me every once in a while in the hall or if my door was open, and he would say, "How are you doing? Are you sure you're going to make it? I can't believe that you are able to come to work. If that happened to me, I would simply fold my tent and hide. I couldn't take it. It's just too painful."

The difference between this other doctor and myself is that I do have a belief system, a bereavement process, so-to-speak, and a confidence that I will see my son again and that he is okay now. This other doctor does not have the benefit of that kind of attitude or approach.

> *It is sometimes not the crisis that upsets us, or the problem itself; it is our mindset, our definition, and how we approach things that really affects us the most.*

Most of us know that good things happen to bad people and bad things happen to good people. That's the way it is. However, I've found that some people fail to understand that there is not a causal relationship between good and bad things happening.

I remember asking one patient, "What causes happiness?"

She remarked quickly, "Sorrow."

I then asked, "What causes pleasure?"

Again she had an instantaneous answer: "Pain."

However, in Matthew 5:45 we are reminded that God is not a respecter of persons, wreaking havoc on some and making flowery paths for others. So as not to pull things out of context, I leave in verses 43 and 44, which teach us our true responsibility of loving our neighbors and of having no prejudices or biases ourselves:

> *Ye have heard that it hath been said, Thou shalt love thy neighbour, and hate thine enemy. But I say unto you, Love your enemies, bless them that curse you, do good to them that hate you, and pray for them which despitefully use you, and persecute you; That ye may be the children of your Father which is in heaven: for he maketh his sun to rise on the evil and on the good, and sendeth rain on the just and on the unjust.*

In my practice I've seen great things come as a result of serious trials. I've also seen great tragedy result from negative and destructive attitudes and behaviors to similar types of problems.

Read these two stories about Sally and Christine and notice how the situations are similar but their experiences were nothing alike:

Seventeen-year-old Sally asked for a conference one evening with her parents. She announced to them that she was pregnant. Needless to say, the parents were disappointed and upset, but Mother's reaction was extraordinary. This brave mother came up, put her arms around her daughter, and told her she loved her. Father followed suit. The next few months involved doctors' appointments, checkups, changes in diet, and sonograms. While the behavior that caused the pregnancy was never condoned, Sally was never rejected. "I'll bet your parents went through the roof," Sally's friends remarked when Sally told them what was going on.

"No," she'd reply. "My parents love me." She was able to explain that they didn't condone her behavior but that they were loving and extending and that they were trying to make the best of the situation. Indeed, it did turn out well. Now, years later, Sally is active in her church, married to a fine man, and the mother of three beautiful children.

Unfortunately, not all stories turn out this well. Many people are scarred, tattered, and alienated for life. In such cases, the crisis becomes a tragedy rather than an opportunity for growth. Consider the following:

A young girl, Christine, became pregnant and her parents were incredibly irate and rejecting. While they did not throw her out of the home, they grudgingly and angrily took her to her doctor appointments, sometimes even delegating this responsibility to her grandmother. Christine endured a lot of contention, ridicule, and constant reprimanding—the "teaching of principles" through haughty lecturing and threatened damnation.

During this process, Christine's pre-school age sister, Penny, was also dragged back and forth to these various appointments. She was highly aware of the contention, anger, and disapproval shown by her parents. On one occasion Penny asked how much longer they would be. Mother sharply said something about Christine just needing to get a shot. The young preschooler broke into tears and cried, "I don't want Christine to get shot. I don't want her to die."

How sad that this five-year-old girl, feeling the extreme censure and anger of the parents toward Christine, was genuinely afraid that her sister was actually going to be shot or executed because of her bad deed.

Both Sally and Christine were in a situation that would dismay any parent. But Sally's parents recognized the need for love and support, and knew that there are worse things in this world than having a baby out of wedlock. Hope existed for them and their daughter. The miracle of creation was taking place within the body of their earthly daughter. These parents knew that "the worth of souls is great in the sight of God" (D&C 18:10). These parents remembered that this child was on loan to them from Heavenly Father. They had taught her correct principles, and they knew that the consequences she was facing were complex and magnified enough that they didn't need to compound her pain. They understood how to show Christ-like love for this child of God.

Christine's parents, on the other hand, seemed to forget all the things that Sally's parents remembered. Indeed, they complicated the suffering of their daughter with constant reminders of her mistake, making caustic and haughty remarks about what a burden this was on them, and derogatory remarks about the situation. Not only was this young woman scarred but her little sister was traumatized. Certainly the baby that was born into this family was facing a much more difficult road to self-esteem, an understanding of the Atonement, and good relationships with the grandparents.

Which type of parent are you? Which type do you hope to be? Sally's parents turned opposition into opportunity. Christine's parents turned opposition into tragedy for themselves, their daughter, and their grandchild.

This earth trek is not easy. Many of us wander, stumble, and get lost as we journey along, seemingly forgetting the iron rod, the great and spacious building in Lehi's dream (see 1 Nephi 8:7–33), and the opportunity we can have to enjoy the companionship of the Holy Ghost to guide us.

Have you seen the picture of the Savior reaching out to all with his arms outstretched? Underneath the picture, the caption reads: "I never said it would be easy; I only said it would be worth it."[8]

OPPORTUNITY

They do me wrong who say I come no more
When once I knock and fail to find you in;
For every day I stand outside your door
And bid you wake, and rise to fight and win.
Wail not for precious chances passed away!
Weep not for golden ages on the wane!
Each night I burn the records of the day—
At sunrise every soul is born again!
Laugh like a boy at splendors that have sped,
To vanished joys be blind and deaf and dumb;
My judgments seal the dead past with its dead,
But never binds a moment yet to come.
Though deep in mire, wring not your hands and weep;
I lend my arm to all who say "I can!"
No shame-faced outcast ever sank so deep
But yet might rise and be again a man!
Dost thou behold thy lost youth all aghast?
Dost thou reel from righteous retribution's blow?
Then turn from the blotted archives of the past
And find the future's pages white as snow.
Art thou a mourner? Rouse thee from thy spell.
Art thou a sinner? Sins may be forgiven;
Each morning gives thee wings to flee from Hell,
Each night a star to guide thy feet to Heaven.[9]

Were Sally and Christine mistakes? Did they make mistakes? What is the difference? Could this situation be a learning, growing, and even a spiritual experience? Of course, we innately know the answer to these questions. Sally and Christine were not mistakes. They had each made a mistake. The difference comes when we keep in mind who we are—children of a loving Heavenly Father and potential deities ourselves, not unforgiven, cast out, and damned souls!

Without a doubt, we will miss out on some blessings. But if we believe Christ can make up for all of our shortcomings and sins, we can get back on the road that leads to our Father in Heaven. We can find joy, even after serious transgressions:

There is a law, irrevocably decreed in heaven before the foundations of the world, upon which all blessings are predicated—and when we obtain any blessing from God, it is by obedience to that law upon which it is predicated. (D&C 130:20-21)

Some members of the Church have unrealistic expectations. Somehow they believe that if they do the right things, they won't experience problems. Remember: good things happen to bad people, and bad things happen to good people. I choose to believe that everything that happens to us can teach us and serve a purpose. Either we or someone close to us can learn a lesson from the things that we encounter.

It took a devastating crisis in my own life to teach me that a terrible experience could also be a learning experience: My parents died when I was a young man, and my brother and sister lived with relatives while I lived with foster parents. In my late teens, I became interested in the gospel of Jesus Christ and eventually served a mission for The Church of Jesus Christ of Latter-day Saints, an event that became a major turning point in my life. After I returned from my mission and married, my wife and I took over the legal guardianship of my fifteen-year-old brother, who was having some difficulties. My brother and I grew very close. He was a son to me because of the guardianship status, as well as a brother and a friend.

When he was seventeen, we moved to Wyoming for graduate work. We had only lived there five weeks when my brother went to a community youth dance where he was beaten to death by four young men. They did not necessarily mean to kill him, but in the fracas, my brother died on the dance floor.

I received a call at 1:30 in the morning by an abrupt, angry-sounding police officer who asked if I was Zane Nelson and if I had a brother by the name of Scott Nelson. I told him I did. He said, "I'm at the Laramie Memorial Hospital with your brother. He dropped dead on a dance floor."

I did not realize until the next day what had happened. I came back from the hospital after identifying my brother's body feeling numb and overwhelmed with confusion and fear. Somehow, I managed to get through the funeral and burial. Later, however, crazed with pain and confusion, I spent many nights screaming out my anger toward God and my parents, whom I felt had abandoned me with a deep and heavy burden.

I finally realized, through the help of one of my professors, that I was giving up. I realized that I had to turn my behaviors around. I was wallowing in self-pity, obsessed with hurt and pain, socially withdrawn, and isolated from others. After a good deal of prayer, my wife and I recognized that the only way I was going to get rid of this depression was to become involved in other things. We made a commitment at that time to missionary work and to the graduate work at hand. As a consequence of real commitment on both our parts, these efforts turned out to be successful.

PAIN STAYED SO LONG

Pain stayed so long I said to him today,
"I will not have you with me any more!"
I stamped my foot and said, "Be on your way,"
And paused there, startled at the look he wore.
"I, who have been your friend," he said to me,
"I, who have been your teacher—all you know
Of understanding, love, of sympathy,
And patience, I have taught you. Shall I go?"
He spoke the truth, this strange unwelcome guest;
I watched him leave, and knew that he was wise.
He left a heart grown tender in my breast,
He left a far, clear vision in my eyes.
I dried my tears, and lifted up a song—
Even for one who'd tortured me so long."[10]

I shudder at this time to think what would have happened to me had I succumbed to that depression and allowed the hurt and pain to control my life. I cannot stress enough that crises will cripple us only when we let them overshadow all other aspects of our lives.

The word *crisis* implies danger and opportunity. Major crises tend to obscure all other problems in the lives of the people affected. A dysfunctional family that centers around a particular person may say, for example, "Gee, we really want to get Dad to stop drinking."

They need to realize, however, that Dad's drinking problem may meet a lot of family needs. While Dad is drinking and dysfunctional, Mom is very busy dealing with Dad's drinking. Kids learn quickly that if they can get one person targeted as the "sicko" then everybody gets off scot-free and they will have to shoulder little, if any, responsibility.

Often, if Dad stops drinking, contention in the family actually increases, at least temporarily, because the parents begin to pay more attention to what the kids are doing. If Dad stops drinking and Mom and Dad get back together and start doing better, all of a sudden Mom and Dad are focusing on questions like, "How well are you doing in school? In your social life? In your moral and religious life?"

Often children don't want this unexpected supervision and even try to split the family again. If the kids can cause enough problems and split the family, Dad might start drinking again, and the focus moves from the children back to the dad.

Splitting is a technique in which an individual adds to a particular distraction that takes the spotlight off him. Children often discover and use this technique; sometimes they're not even aware that they are doing it. It can also happen in organizations or in extended family relationships.

Once I had a young female patient in the psychiatric ward of a local hospital. She managed, through her manipulation, to get everybody—her parents, her doctors, the staff at the hospital—all upset with one another, and she was able to skate free of her responsibilities. I called a meeting with the key staff and her parents and asked, "Who's the patient here?" They replied that it was this young girl who was down watching a movie with the other adolescents. "So why," I asked, "if she is the patient, are we having this meeting?"

As we talked, it became obvious that everybody was angry with one another and that this young patient had been the instigator of many of the problems, causing us to become distracted so she could "skate free."

People use the following three techniques to cause splitting:

1. **Quoting Out of Context:** The quote may be accurate. It just may be part of one sentence out of perhaps a four-page dissertation. For example, this young girl in the hospital was asked to wear certain signs around her neck that reflected some of her manipulative behaviors. She told me and her parents that her counselor had said the signs were stupid. His quote was accurate, but he said a lot more than that and, put in context, his comment was certainly not anti-therapeutic. However, the patient had used the quote successfully to distract us and get out of wearing the signs.

2. **Exaggeration:** People use words like *never, always,* and *every time.* They tend to exaggerate a situation to a point that everybody becomes angry with one another. For example, this young girl would

say things like, "Dr. Nelson never sees me." "The nurses ignore me." "Dr. _____ went down the hall and never acknowledged me." These overstatements upset her parents as well as staff personnel at the hospital. She also talked about Bruce, a young psych tech, whom she was smitten by, as being the only one who ever really understood her and her needs and concerns. Consequently, I got upset. With all of us upset, she again got to skate free.

3.   Good Guy, Bad Guy: A person accomplishes this by building up one person's self-esteem, which often implies criticism of another. "Gee, it's great having somebody who really understands me," this girl told a younger counselor. "You're wonderful." This made the counselor feel good but also made her subtly angry at me. Eventually, I felt this anger and was frustrated and upset because I didn't know what was causing it. Again, the patient got to skate out of her responsibility.

Such splitting techniques are common. People use these techniques to distract others, divert the spotlight, and encourage other people to start negatively interacting with one another. It's a destructive process and one in which, in a way, everybody becomes a victim. Recognizing this technique can help us stop our ugly dances and interactions.

Crises can even become a way of life for some people. While this book is partially intended to help people deal more effectively with various crises, it also teaches how to head off crises before they happen. While learning crisis-management skills is certainly helpful, avoiding crises altogether can enrich our lives and make us happier and healthier.

Obviously, then, crisis situations are not the only times when we can change. The book of Acts contains a moving description of a change of heart in the story of the Saints' conversion before and after Peter and John were arrested. The Saints were not only of one heart, but they also lived with all things in common, reflective of what we have heard described as the United Order (see Acts 4:32–35). That would be difficult under ideal circumstances. Most of know all too well that petty pride, selfishness, laziness, and discouragement are powerful tools in Satan's arsenal against us.

Many times people have said to me, "The closer I get to doing what's right, the more Satan works on me." Well, of course he does! He doesn't want anything good to go on in your life or mine. The more chaos and pain in our families, the better Satan likes it, the more comfortable he is that we've got ourselves so messed up that we think we won't be able to work our way out of it. Thankfully, the plan of Heavenly Father disputes that. We can change.

We can make it through those tests and we can develop and display self-esteem, humility, faith, determination, compassion, and toughness. Best of all, we can even have fun along the way.

Believing in quick fixes with little or no effort is Satan's idea. Some of us have a lottery mentality (immediate fix) or soap opera mentality (problems solved during a half-hour television program). Life's problems aren't usually like that, and thinking that quick fixes will work is actually a quick way of making things seem okay when they really aren't. Nevertheless, millions buy into this way of thinking. Unfortunately, very few ever really solve their problems with this approach. Being willing to work hard and sacrifice are the only sure ways to gain success. With that attitude adjustment, there is and always will be help from on high.

FOOTPRINTS IN THE SAND

One night a man had a dream.

He dreamed he was walking along the beach with the Lord.

Across the sky flashed scenes from his life.

For each scene, he noticed two sets of footprints in the sand;

One belonged to him, and the other to the Lord.

When the last scene of his life flashed before him,

He looked back at the footprints in the sand.

He noticed that many times along the path of his life

There was only one set of footprints.

He also noted that it happened at the very lowest

And saddest times of his life.

This really bothered him and he questioned the Lord about it.

"Lord, you said that once I decided to follow you,

You'd walk with me all the way.

But I have noticed that during the most troublesome times

In my life, there is only one set of footprints.

I don't understand why when I needed you most

You would leave me."

The Lord replied, "My precious child,

I love you and I would never leave you.

During your times of trial and suffering,
When you see only one set of footprints,
It was then that I carried you."[11]

One speaker noted, "I am convinced that God allows friction and abrasion to happen to us in order to help us grow. Sometimes these trials can grow to true crisis proportions, but when they do, we must compel ourselves: "If life hands you lemons, make lemonade."[12]

Another of my favorite quotes states:

> *Moving parts in rubbing contact require lubrication to avoid excessive wear. Honorifics and formal politeness provide lubrication where people rub together. Often the very young, the untraveled, the naive, the unsophisticated, deplore these formalities as "empty," "meaningless," or "dishonest," and scorn to use them. No matter how "pure" their motives, they thereby throw sand into machinery that does not work too well at best.*[13]

We can also learn a valuable lesson from the oyster. If it were not for that little grain of sand that gets into an oyster's shell, the oyster would never create one of the most beautiful gems we have on this earth. That irritation, that opposition, is used to its very best possibility by the little oyster. A pearl is actually "a dense concretion, lustrous and varying in color, formed as an abnormal growth within the shell of some mollusks."[14] What beautiful pearl each adversity becomes!

Likewise, we have all known amazing people who turn tragedy into triumph and come off victorious amid extreme circumstances. What gives them mental toughness and the character necessary to overcome? I believe one of the key things they have done (in all cases) is that they have quit making excuses and have accepted the responsibility for who they are and what they will amount to in this life.

Could it be true, then, that excuses are useless? Let's see.

Chapter Three

NEVER BE ACCOUNTABLE— WALLOW IN SELF-PITY

EACH ONE OF US CAME into this world with a perfect excuse to fail. We were born to mortal parents who made mistakes. As a result, many people have found it desirable as well as advantageous to blame their mistakes, errors, and misfortunes on our parents. Furthermore, it is socially acceptable to blame our poor grades in school, our failures in relationships, and our smoking, drinking, swearing, and dishonesty on our substandard upbringing. Why not? There are a few heroes out there, but why try to rise above mediocrity? Why not wallow in the mire in which our parents, siblings, environment, and social status have surrounded us? The world owes us better than that . . . right? We are entitled to certain things . . . right?

Wrong!

Life's victims fail to consider one important thing—their agency, or the power to choose. None of us was born with a monitor to tell our parents exactly what we needed and when we needed it, but our parents faced the challenges of taking care of a little person that they knew little or nothing about.

We are blessed to live in the information age. Just think of the complexity of taking care of an infant before the great age of Dr. Spock, *Blue's Clues*, and *Sesame Street*.

Our ancestors were certainly disadvantaged without the "blessings" of video games, over-crowded schools, uncensored Internet, and grandparents who would raise their grandchildren so today's young families could have more toys, more vacations, and nicer cars. The X and Me generations have learned well the incidental lessons from these and other modern amenities. I see youth on both the high and low ends of the dollar sign who are often rebellious, disobedient, fit-throwing troublemakers who have adopted an attitude of taking responsibility for nothing and passing the buck for everything else.

Parents come to me frustrated because despite their best efforts, it seems that delayed gratification and goal setting have been thrown out the window. Many of today's youth want things now, receive things too quickly, and appreciate almost nothing. The focus is on novelty, stimulation, and excitement. At an early age, their world becomes full of organized activities such as soccer, baseball, and scouts. Sometimes young people get so many activities going that the mother looks like a frazzled taxi-cab driver and the kids are anxious and nervous, pushed to go here and there. They do not know how to entertain themselves. Often, if left to their own demise, they get in trouble. The 4:20 study (as it is sometimes referred to) shows that most children get into trouble at 4:20 in the afternoon when they are unsupervised and left with unstructured time.

One of my sons, at the age of twelve years old, was caught in an interesting double-bind one Saturday morning. He had a soccer game that he wanted to play in, and there was a scout activity at the same time. He, so-to-speak, blew a gasket and complained that it wasn't fair, it wasn't right, and how could he make a choice. Double-bound, he threw his arms up in despair and cried.

In contrast, of advantages and disadvantages, many of us are familiar with the story of Helen Keller. She was a normal child who at the age of eighteen months was plunged into a world of darkness and silence. This amazing, unfortunate girl raised herself, literally, from a world of emptiness and misunderstanding to a world of light, sound, insight, sensitivity, intelligence and joy!

In her early years, experts advised her parents that institutionalizing Helen was the only available option. A child with one handicap was difficult enough, but one with a handicap of both sight and sound was "unteach-able." At the age of seven, Helen experienced "the most important day of [her] life." That was when twenty-year-old Annie Sullivan came to be her teacher. The two were inseparable until Annie's death in 1936.

Helen graduated from Radcliffe University cum laude in 1904. Annie finger spelled into Helen's hand countless references and other types of books as well as lectures. In addition to her own biography, Ms. Keller wrote eleven other books. In 1936, Helen Keller moved to Westport, Connecticut, where she lived until her death on June 1, 1968, at the age of eighty-seven. In his eulogy at her funeral, Senator Lister Hill noted, "[Helen] will live on, one of the few, immortal names not born to die. Her spirit will endure as long as man can read and stories can be told of the woman who showed the world there are no boundaries to courage and faith."[15]

What made Ms. Keller achieve so much? Why didn't she just give up when all the odds were against her? Why didn't she blame God, genetics, and her parents for her misfortune? Why did she think she could rise above her circumstances?

These are good questions, and answering them should be both thought provoking and insightful.

Many of us spend time saying "why Lord?" and "why me, Lord?" Instead of questions like these, maybe we can take the advice given in the following poem and capitalize on the power through adversity that life's lessons and experiences teach us.

POIGNANT THOUGHT

They say that knowledge is power.
But knowledge is just information.
For power to come from your knowledge
You must meet it with observation.
Peruse it, review it, and pray.
Hope that wisdom may come from these facts.
But the truth without application
And mere whimsy will govern your acts.
We must apply the things we learn
For every experience is pricey.
Unless we value what we've gone through
Our advice is no more than dicey!
But if we seek with true fervor . . .

A wise mentor may teach us the way.
So we will grow from what has been taught
And not throw all those lessons away.[16]

Do we apply what we have learned or do we keep making the same mistake over and over? Or, do we make one mistake after another? There is a difference! If you keep making the same mistake over and over, you aren't learning anything from the experience. However, if you keep making one mistake after another, that may mean progress! Crisis is defined as "that change in a disease that indicates whether the result is to be recovery or death."[17]

In a very real sense, crisis actually means danger and opportunity.

This brings us to society's attitude of entitlement, or a way of thinking that allows anyone who is having a difficult time to cry "foul!" From this point of view, if we are not doing as well as our next door neighbor, we are underprivileged and we deserve help. Someone needs to take care of us!

I'm often asked about the leading cause of suicide. Feelings of helplessness and, even more importantly, hopelessness, kill effort. Most of the time we can see some end to our sorrow or pain, or at least we feel we can do something about it through sheer determination. When we lock ourselves into feeling that we have little or no power over life, we are actually accepting a victim script. Feelings of hopelessness kill effort, and effort is absolutely essential to growth, regardless of the state of mental health.

It takes effort and accountability to help ourselves and others.

"You cannot lift another soul," President Harold B. Lee said, "until you are standing on higher ground than he is. You must be sure, if you would rescue the man, that you yourself are setting the example of what you would have him be. You cannot light a fire in another soul unless it is burning in your own soul."[18]

Some men will wheel their children or wives into mental health professionals with the attitude, "I can't fix them; you do it." They may be disgusted and frustrated, but my job is to try to convince these husbands to make the effort, to join me and the other members of their families in working toward understanding and resolution instead of allowing the husbands to withdraw and say, "Make 'em right, and I'll pick 'em up when you're done."

"Disciplining our children and holding them accountable for their actions does not mean we do not forgive them," I read in a Christmas letter I received one year. "Nor do we have some kind of grudge or hatred for them by so disciplining them. It is necessary for their welfare, for their family, and for society. Hatred or lack of forgiveness motivates no desire to be accountable. Anarchy, resentment, and abject fear stare us in the face if we equate forgiveness with freeing people from their moral obligations and accountability to the law. Without punishment, the law is meaningless."[19]

God is bound by rules and regulations, as are we. His will does not always occur. Not all of the blessings promised in the scriptures come to pass because there is a hook or stipulation. Perhaps the phrase "through your righteousness," "through your faithfulness," or "through our good works" is tacked on the end. The blessings will come if we do certain things. God too is bound by natural laws that preclude him from forcing people.

> *Wherefore, men are free according to the flesh; and all things are given them which are expedient unto man. And they are free to choose liberty and eternal life, through the great Mediator of all men, or to choose captivity and death, according to the captivity and power of the devil; for he seeketh that all men might be miserable like unto himself.* (2 Nephi 2:27)

Sometimes people experience havoc or injuries caused by other people. Our Heavenly Father does not prevent all of these things from happening. Likewise, He doesn't cause them; rather He allows them to happen as a result of agency, ours or someone else's. People have a right to mess up their lives. Unfortunately, many times innocent victims result along the way. But, the agency is still their own. We fought a war in heaven about that, didn't we?

In the Doctrine and Covenants, we are taught about agency and intelligence, and we are warned by the Lord:

> *All truth is independent in that sphere in which God has placed it, to act for itself, as all intelligence also; otherwise there is no existence. Behold, here is the agency of man, and here is the condemnation of man; because that which was from the beginning is plainly manifest unto them, and they*

*receive not the light. And every man whose spirit receiveth
not the light is under condemnation.* (D&C 93:30–32)

Let me tell you another story from Greek mythology: Orestes was
a mortal man. He returned from being exiled as a child to find that his
father had been murdered and that his mother had already remarried.
Orestes was told by Apollo that he had a responsibility to find out who
murdered his father and to kill that person. Orestes found out that it
was his mother who actually killed his father. Orestes was caught in an
interesting double bind. To perform matricide was a terrible damnation.
However, not to avenge the death of one's father was also a terrible damnation. Consequently, it was a classical double bind: Damned if you do,
damned if you don't.

Orestes chose to kill his mother and therefore was damned. The gods
sent upon Orestes furies and harpies (anxieties) and auditory hallucina-
tions. Orestes was in hell. Apollo saw the hell that Orestes was in and
also saw the double bind in which he had placed Orestes. Apollo asked
for a trial or hearing of the gods. Apollo pled Orestes's case, pointing out
the double bind and how Orestes couldn't win. Orestes sprang to his feet
screaming, "Enough. I knew what I was doing, and I take responsibility."

The gods were so impressed that Orestes would take responsibility, or even that any man would take on such responsibility, that they
completely forgave Orestes. The harpies and the furies were turned into
amenities or niceties.[20]

From this story we learn about responsibility—and the origin of
certain words: *harpies, furies,* and *amenities.* We can also recognize
that, unlike Orestes, mortal humans, in general, use all kinds of ways
to resist taking responsibility. Some ways, often called ego defense
mechanisms, include projection, rationalization, minimization, and
denial. Most of us know what it is to rationalize, deny, and minimize.
But what is projection?

Projection is an unconscious ego defense mechanism in which
a person finds his or her thoughts, ideas, feelings, and impulses are so
undesirable or unacceptable that he projects those unacceptable traits or
thoughts onto someone else—and then judges and blames that person.
Often, the person doing the projecting isn't even aware that he had those
unacceptable thoughts or feelings in the first place.

When I perform a mental status examination, two tasks—insight and
judgment—play a critical role. In other words, when something negative

or positive happens, does someone have the insight to say, "Aha! Now I get it!"? Judgment is tougher to define—and recognize. Judgment involves a person not only realizing why something happened but also applying that experience in his life so a desired outcome occurs in the future.

Many people feel as if they are victims. They claim they are not responsible or accountable for how their lives have turned out. However, recognition of the principles and the extent that we are truly accountable in God's eyes is essential for complete mental health. Distortion and disillusionment do not free us from our culpability, responsibility, or accountability. They make reasonable-sounding excuses; they make scintillating topics of conversation. But a just and righteous God knows more than just what happened to each of us during our lives. He knows the condition of our hearts. He knows whether we would have made different choices if given different circumstances. He knows, even if we do not, the true heart of every person.

I like the study of behavioral therapy. Behavioral therapy puts individual responsibility where it belongs. Too many of us license our behaviors. If somebody has ever hurt us, we feel vindicated in acting negatively in return. The last ten verses of Matthew 5 refute that approach. If we react as the natural man, we will never win.

In essence, it does not matter what other people do to us. It comes down to what we do and how we react to what others do.

> *I am not responsible for whether other people like me; I am only responsible for whether I like them.*[21]

This philosophy can be taken even further as a close friend relayed to me recently: "I am not responsible for whether other people hurt me in any way; I am, however, responsible to make certain that I do not hurt them."

Without doubt, I have never learned anything in psychology more profound or powerful than "The Serenity Prayer." The Serenity Prayer was originally part of a speech given by Reinhold Niebuhr, a popular Christian speaker during World War II. The Serenity Prayer was taken from one of his speeches and shared with many of the military personnel during World War II. Reverend Neibuhr's beautiful poem has been misquoted much of the time, and his family has worked diligently to get the word out as to the common errors in the poem that most of us have heard.

Heard mostly in an abbreviated form, I quote it here correctly in its entirety according to Reverend Neibuhr's biography:

THE SERENITY PRAYER

God, give us grace to accept with serenity
the things that cannot be changed,
courage to change the things
which should be changed,
and the wisdom to distinguish
the one from the other.
Living one day at a time,
Enjoying one moment at a time,
Accepting hardship as a pathway to peace,
Taking, as Jesus did,
This sinful world as it is,
Not as I would have it.
Trusting that You will make all things right,
If I surrender to Your will,
So that I may be reasonably happy in this life,
And supremely happy with You forever in the next.
Amen.[22]

An insightful Christian woman once said to me, "Most Christians are too pharisaical. They are so concerned about doing things absolutely right that they won't make any decisions on their own. They have to have someone else (an authority figure) tell them what to do." After thinking about her comments and reflecting on my service in leadership positions within the Church, I felt that what she said was true. Christ had been critical of the Pharisees, in part, because of their rigidity.

Many of us want a manual to tell us all the moves we should make; we want someone to tell us exactly how we should think, feel, and act. We often fail to realize the harm such a manual would do to individuality and imagination. Indeed, we know that:

> It is not meet that [the Lord] should command in all things;
> for he that is compelled in all things, the same is a slothful
> and not a wise servant; wherefore he receiveth no reward.
> (D&C 58:26)

To be commanded in all things would negate the growth that is possible through the exercise of agency. Why do so many of us seek for guidance or counseling on almost everything we do? Do we want direction so that we will have someone to blame if things go wrong? Do we want direction because we are incapable of making our own decisions, our mental insufficiencies not allowing us to think things through clearly enough to make a decision?

Do we think it matters to Heavenly Father whether we become a tax consultant or a store owner, a psychologist or a policeman, a welder or a teacher? Our Heavenly Father has said that He is "no respecter of persons" (Ephesians 6:9; see also D&C 1:35). He wants all of us to make correct, mature, responsible decisions and return to live with Him. But, having said that, He tells us in these same scriptures that "the day speedily cometh when peace shall be taken from the earth, and the devil shall have power over his own dominion," or those who have chosen to follow him. Likewise, "the Lord shall have power over his saints, and shall reign in their midst, and shall come down in judgment upon Idumea, or the world" (D&C 1:36). The Lord winds up this counsel by saying:

> *What I the Lord have spoken, I have spoken, and I excuse not myself; and though the heavens and the earth pass away, my word shall not pass away, but shall all be fulfilled, whether by mine own voice or by the voice of my servants, it is the same.* (D&C 1:38)

I like this quote from Rita Mae Brown:

> *Good judgment comes from experience and often, experience comes from bad judgment."*

Do we learn from the experiences of others, or do we have to learn everything first-hand? Let's consider the story of Job. As I read this story, several things impress me:

• During the earlier years of his life, when everything was going well, Job had many friends, a happy family, and high esteem within the community.

• Jehovah knew Job better than Satan did. Jehovah was confident in Job's loyalty, righteousness, and testimony, while Satan had no confidence in Job at all and reveled in the idea that he could make Job fall. He even teased and tempted the Lord, telling Him that Job was only faithful because he had been blessed so abundantly. Satan told the Lord that if Job's blessings were taken away from him, Job would curse God to His face.

• When Job's trials began to be evident, even his wife told him to "curse God, and die" (Job 2:9). Job's friends, who originally came to mourn with him, turned on him almost immediately and asked him what he had done to bring upon him the judgments of God.

• Those same friends assumed that he was no longer righteous because he was apparently being punished by God.

• Job went through the full process of healing. He experienced shock, anger, sadness, humility, understanding, acceptance, and even gratitude for his suffering.

• As a consequence, he "pulled himself up by the boot straps"[23] and refused to wallow in self-pity. He moved on with faith and trust in the Lord, and as a result, he grew from his trials and was a better man for having endured them.

This growth through adversity was not something that only Job would go through. In fact, each one of us may be the benefactor of such experiences.

President Spencer W. Kimball, twelfth president of The Church of Jesus Christ of Latter-day Saints, endured many physical trials and much adversity during his life. Like Job, he was wracked with pain from severe boils his entire life. He endured many illnesses, including typhoid fever and small pox, and experienced multiple surgeries as a result of a failing heart, cerebral hemorrhages, and so forth. He fought recurring throat cancer with the removal of all but one of his vocal cords, which virtually guaranteed that he would never speak or sing again. He beat those odds, however, and developed a raspy voice, which allowed him to speak again.[24]

I wonder if we knew how much we actually benefited from our trials, if we might not ask for more. Certainly most of us would never dream of praying for more trials, but we often pray for greater faith and stronger backs, and these often come as we face and overcome trials. Albert Einstein said:

> We cannot solve our problems with the same thinking we
> used when we created them.[25]

Certainly Einstein's deep understanding for problem-solving couldn't have been any greater than Mother Teresa's understanding of trials and suffering. She related the following story:

> *I was consoling a little girl who was sick and had much pain. I told her, "You should be happy that God sends you suffering, because your sufferings are a proof that God loves you much. Your sufferings are kisses from Jesus." "Then, Mother," answered the little girl, "please ask Jesus not to kiss me so much."*[26]

To wrap up this chapter, I found this thought-provoking autobiography:

AUTOBIOGRAPHY IN FIVE SHORT CHAPTERS

Chapter 1
I walk down the street.
There is a deep hole in the sidewalk.
I fall in . . . I am lost . . . I am helpless . . .
It isn't my fault.
It takes forever to find a way out.

Chapter 2
I walk down the same street.
There is a deep hole in the sidewalk.
I pretend I don't see it.
I fall in again. I can't believe I am in this same place.
But it isn't my fault. It still takes a long time to get out.

Chapter 3
I walk down the same street.
There is a deep hole in the sidewalk. I see it is there.
I still fall in . . . it's a habit . . . but my eyes are open.
I know where I am. It is my fault, my responsibility.
I get out immediately.

Chapter 4
I walk down the same street.
There is a hole in the sidewalk.
I walk around it.

Chapter 5
I walk down another street.[27]

My hope is that each of us will see the things in our attitudes that paralyze us or keep us from reaching our full potential.

If it's to be, it's up to me.[28]

I hope that each of us will come to the realization that life is a journey not a destination—and then discover that the journey is the best part.

Chapter Four

USE INCORRECT METHODS TO TEACH CORRECT PRINCIPLES

I ONCE WORKED WITH A couple who had been married more than twenty years. Both had been married before, and both had children from their first marriages. Over time, this couple had developed many hurts and were living separate lives; there was an obvious physical and mental separation. When the families were together, the children and grandchildren were forced to focus on one or the other of the couple because they couldn't even speak politely when they were in a room together.

Personal involvement uncovered many of the things that had caused unrelenting pain and bad feelings. He was a strict straight-liner and saw everything in terms of right and wrong, black and white. He had no flexibility. On Sundays, they took separate vehicles to church because the wife came home after the first meeting. The husband constantly reprimanded her for not staying for all three meetings. He implied that they had financial trouble because of her lack of righteousness and unwillingness to serve. He told the adult children that she didn't have a temple recommend because she didn't pay a full tithing. He would bash her and justify himself with scriptures and principles that made her feel bad and caused resentment.

While they didn't divorce, they were estranged and alienated from each other during the last several years of the husband's life.

While it is certainly right to study the scriptures, go to church on Sunday, keep the Sabbath day holy, pay tithing, pray, and pursue many other righteous endeavors, using these principles as the basis for condemnation, belittling, or chastising another is not what our Heavenly Father intended.

Let's face it—spouses are imperfect and our children are at times self-centered, amoral, narcissistic, or incredibly self-involved. I sometimes tease that we probably would have drowned them at birth had we known what we were getting into.

Nevertheless, we are where we are. Let's start there.

> *Most of the problems you will have in your life you will either have married or given birth to.*[29]

In teaching correct principles to those we're involved with, we have to realize that these principles are correct for us. We are trying to get our own point of view across. Sometimes the things we are trying so desperately to teach are, in and of themselves, wrong! Yet, I have never met a parent who deliberately tried to teach his children errant thinking or behavior. I haven't had any parents come in who didn't want their children to be hardworking, honest, self-reliant, and moral. However, is there a best way to influence them to be that way?

A PARENT'S LOVE

I gave you life,
but cannot live it for you.
I can teach you things,
but I cannot make you learn.
I can give you directions,
but I cannot be there to lead you.
I can allow you freedom,
but I cannot account for it.
I can take you to church,
but I cannot make you believe.
I can teach you right from wrong,
but I cannot always decide for you.
I can buy you beautiful clothes,

but I cannot make you beautiful inside.
I can offer you advice,
but I cannot accept it for you.
I can give you love,
but I cannot force it upon you.
I can teach you to share,
but I cannot make you unselfish.
I can teach you respect,
but I cannot force you to show honor.
I can advise you about friends,
but cannot choose them for you.
I can advise you about sex,
but I cannot keep you pure.
I can tell you the facts of life,
but I can't build your reputation.
I can tell you about drinking,
but I can't say "no" for you.
I can warn you about drugs,
but I can't prevent you from using them.
I can tell you about lofty goals,
but I can't achieve them for you.
I can teach you about kindness,
but I can't force you to be gracious.
I can warn you about sins,
but I cannot make you moral.
I can love you as a child,
but I cannot place you in God's family.
I can pray for you,
but I cannot make you walk with God.
I can teach you about Jesus,
but I cannot make Jesus your Lord.
I can tell you how to live,
but I cannot give you eternal life.
I can love you with unconditional love all of my
life . . . and I will![30]

Repetition is one of our best teachers, but as we look at our associations with others, particularly with our children and grandchildren, we discover that there are three variables that affect the significance of most associations and relationships more than anything else:

- Frequency of interaction
- Duration of interaction
- Intensity of interaction

In looking at these variables, we realize that many people with whom we may have frequent contact, and whom we may have known for a long time, have not affected us very much. However, some people have affected us significantly, and we may barely be acquainted with them. Perhaps we don't see them frequently or have never met them at all. Certainly Jesus was one of these influential people.

Out of these three variables, intensity determines how much credence, belief, and identification we place in that relationship or association. While all of these variables are certainly important, if you have to choose between frequency, duration, and intensity, we should never sacrifice intensity.

However, when it comes to convincing people of our beliefs or opinions, whatever they may be, three additional factors come into play:

- Logos: the logic—that is, how much reason, how well thought out, is the general logic of the argument.
- Pathos: the emotion (positive or negative) behind the argument. Certainly we have seen others present anger and frustration versus love and gentleness while trying to argue a point or teach a principle.
- Ethos: the credibility the presenter has with those listening.

The teaching process requires two or more people:

1. A teacher
2. At least one participating student

You'll notice that I didn't say "lecturing" requires two or more people. No, lecturing is different from teaching. Teaching involves a person who shares knowledge with someone else for that other person's benefit. It also involves the willing participation of the person filling the role of a student. A lecturer prepares information and disseminates that information in a designated form and time frame.

A good teacher, however, prepares information and looks for teaching moments that benefit both the student and the teacher. Good teachers don't say too much—or too little—yet they edify those who are listening. A good teacher uses multiple methods to teach, realizing that some students are visual learners, some are verbal learners, some are kinetic learners and others are a combination.

Correct principles can be some of the most frustrating concepts to teach or instill in others. Correct principles can be confused with the terms laws, rules, or commandments. But a principle is so much more than a law, rule, or commandment.

People sometimes have a difficult time with abstract or complex thinking. For example, take the old adage "avoid the appearance of evil," which is derived from 1 Thessalonians 5:22. This concept may sound simple to many of us, but it is amazing how many people do not fully grasp it. Several of the Savior's parables were complex, for even his own disciples. On one occasion, they didn't understand the parable of the sower and asked what it meant. He answered:

> *Unto you it is given to know the mysteries of the kingdom of God: but to others in parables; that seeing they may not see, and hearing they might not understand.* (Luke 8:10)

The proverbs, parables, and adages that you and I grew up with are abstract and easily misunderstood. Consider the following:

- A watched pot never boils.
- Penny wise, dollar foolish.
- Time is money.
- People who live in glass houses should not throw stones.
- Don't put all your eggs in one basket.
- Avoid the appearance of evil.
- A bird in the hand is worth two in the bush.
- A stitch in time saves nine.
- All good things come to he who waits.
- Don't judge a book by its cover.
- If at first you don't succeed, try, try again.

Then, from the Ten Commandments:

- Thou shalt not bear false witness against thy neighbour.
- Honour thy father and thy mother.
- Thou shalt not steal.

- Thou shalt not covet thy neighbour's house, thou shalt not covet thy neighbour's wife, nor his manservant, nor his maidservant, nor his ox, nor his ass, nor any thing that is thy neighbour's.
- Thou shalt not commit adultery.
- Remember the Sabbath day, to keep it holy.

Sometimes we think we understand the commandments, but, we might ask ourselves, what is the difference between lying and gossiping? Between shoplifting and plagiarism? Between adultery and fornication? Between admiring and coveting?

We all have little holes or blind spots of naïveté in our vision. I do not have the ability to create art; I simply do not have spatial ability. Some people have a very difficult time with math and cannot learn many math concepts. We all have our strengths and weaknesses. The problem is some people struggle to learn empathy, sympathy, and conscience, and therefore, they are in a tough corner. They often end up in prisons or on probation or become institutionalized in other ways.

Indeed, society insists that people have a reasonable amount of principles, but those without sympathy, empathy, and conscience are just clueless. If a young man with this problem, for example, broke into your house and stole a shotgun that had been in the family for several generations, cut the stock off, cut the barrels off, broke it apart, and got caught afterward, he would exhibit no remorse. You might explain to him how precious this gun was to your family, that it wasn't just the financial value but that it was an heirloom passed down through many generations. This young man would probably stare at you and say, "It's just a shotgun." The fact is they just really don't comprehend remorse, sympathy, empathy, or sensitivity.

Sometimes we call such people sociopaths, schizoid personalities, anti-social personalities, and dissociative personalities. But I actually think these struggles are like learning disabilities. If we say that these are learning disabilities, is a person unable to learn these concepts, or is society unable to grasp them or instill them? Sociologists call a person's failure to learn these concepts anomia, and their culture's or society's inability or failure to teach these concepts anomie.

Psychiatric units often try to help people understand abstract thinking using abstract examples. Yet some people are simply incapable of doing that. They may be gifted in some other area such as music or math, so clearly they aren't lacking intelligence, but abstraction and common sense appear to go beyond their abilities.

Therefore, sometimes a strict behavioral approach is critical and necessary. For instance, if you told certain people to keep the Sabbath day holy, they would have no idea what that meant. The idea is too ambiguous and abstract for them. Instead, they need to be told specifically what they can and can't do on the Sabbath. Another example might be if you were to tell a child or teen with a blind spot in this area of his thinking to be respectful, he would have no idea what you are talking about.

Picture an electric circuit. As long as there is no break in a circuit, the light fixture or appliance functions. However, if there is a break anywhere in the circuit, the light or appliance cannot receive electricity. The break must be found and the circuit completed before the electricity is able to complete its function. That's how our thinking might be if we don't have appropriate boundaries or if we are dealing with abandonment issues, abuse, or even monetary challenges from our childhood. Sometimes people even have these gaps in their circuitry when they have grown up in the best of circumstances. Whatever the reason for the gap or break in circuitry, telling someone to be respectful when he has this gap would be as effective as telling him to grow feathers!

Whether these individuals want specific instructions or not, they have to be told exactly what the words *respect* and *appropriate* mean. They need to know the following rules:

- Don't touch another person without permission.
- Don't take things that don't belong to you.
- Don't put your feet on furniture.
- Don't pinch or hit.

To most of us, respect would equal these things. However, if this is where your gap exists, you won't be able to compute the meaning of the word; it simply doesn't add up. The inability has nothing to do with being good or bad, smart or stupid; it is simply a break in a certain "circuit," or way of thinking, that requires specific instruction.

Another common area where thinking errors may occur is emotional blackmail or anything a person does to give him an unfair advantage over someone else. The action can be anything that offends, intimidates, threatens, or persuades, but it is something that tips the scale in a person's favor. Unrighteous dominion may be practiced by many who are older or even by children who throw tantrums or use other controlling behavior.

I was counseling a woman who was ready to file for divorce because she was tired of her husband's intimidating behavior. He had never hit her, but she was afraid of him. He had a way of communicating that made her afraid. When I discussed emotional blackmail with him and indicated he needed to stop using it, he slammed his hand down onto the table, and screamed, "I don't use emotional blackmail!" He had a pen in his hand, which he threw down as well. He had no idea what emotional blackmail was, even though we had discussed it several times.

To get his attention—and to show him what he was doing—I took the pen I was holding, slammed it down on the table, and shouted, "So you don't use emotional blackmail, huh!?" This surprised him so much that he recognized and even learned to correct his behaviors.

My actions were a radical attempt to help him see the way he had been intimidating his wife and children. He had a deep desire to repair his family, and once he understood emotional blackmail, he recognized that he would often stand over his wife and children or get in their faces and raise his voice. He didn't hit anyone, but he was a large and powerful man, and the threat was real. At times he even moved toward his children with a broom, a spoon, or even a finger pointed in their faces, along with loud, intimidating instructions.

EMOTIONAL BLACKMAIL CAN INCLUDE:

- Shouting
- Stomping
- Pounding
- Throwing things
- Slamming doors
- Hyper-conrolling of others
- Strictness
- Ranting and raving
- Slapping
- Glaring
- Ignoring
- Waving or holding potential weapons
- Rolling eyes
- Loud sighing
- Name calling
- Sarcasm
- Snide laughing

- Pushing
- Blocking movement or doorways
- Verbal threatening (suicide, self-inflicted injury, victims)
- Forceful sexual activity

This forty-year-old man needed to learn new information so that he could complete the circuit of correct thinking and appropriate behavior in this area. Not surprisingly, various children in the family had tendencies to deal with conflict and opposition as they had seen their father do. We had several family counseling sessions, and over time, with consistent and appropriate reinforcement, this family became much stronger. They were able to identify and target misbehavior in each other and, in a non-threatening way, encourage change. I see great hope for the next generation of this family to be more mentally healthy.

Each of us impacts everyone else we come into contact with for good or bad. Whether we like it or not, we are all examples, role models, and teachers. Whether or not we know we are being watched, children, teenagers, and other adults are forming ideas, developing standards, and patterning their thoughts and behaviors because of things they see us do and hear us say.

Once, in a Sacrament meeting, the speaker said, "My job, as I see it, is to speak to you for twenty minutes. Your job is to listen to me for twenty minutes. If you get done before I do, let me know."

As parents, we have all seen that glassy stare come over our children's eyes when they are done listening but we aren't done talking. At that point, we might as well be speaking a foreign language because they aren't going to pick up any more information. Many times parents tell me that they are praying that their child will do this or that. I have a suggestion that may be more appropriate. Instead of praying that David will want to go on a mission, pray that he will have a desire to serve the Lord. In desiring to serve the Lord, he will probably choose to go on a mission, but he will also desire to attend his meetings, honor his priesthood, and pay a full tithing. While they may sound very similar, one is a specific request while one encompasses everything that David does, now and in the future.

As another example, instead of praying that Molly will end her relationship with her live-in boyfriend, pray that she will have a desire to be a worthy example to her younger brothers and sisters. Can you see the subtle differences? One is specific and the other is broad. The one may bring around that specific event, but the other may change the course and path of numerous lives.

MEMORANDUM FROM YOUR CHILD

1. Don't spoil me. I know quite well that I ought not to have all I ask for. I'm only testing you.
2. Don't be afraid to be firm with me. I prefer it; it makes me feel secure.
3. Don't let me form bad habits. I have to rely on you to detect them in the early stages.
4. Don't make me feel smaller than I am. It only makes me behave stupidly "big."
5. Don't correct me in front of people. I'll take much more notice if you talk quietly with me in private.
6. Don't make me feel that my mistakes are sins. It upsets my sense of values.
7. Don't protect me from consequences. I need to learn the painful way sometimes.
8. Don't be too upset when I say "I hate you." Sometimes it isn't you I hate but your power to thwart me.
9. Don't take too much notice of my small ailments. Sometimes they get me the attention I need.
10. Don't nag. If you do, I shall have to protect myself by appearing deaf.
11. Don't forget that I cannot explain myself as well as I should like. That is why I am not always accurate.
12. Don't put me off when I ask questions. If you do, you will find that I stop asking and seek my information elsewhere.
13. Don't be inconsistent. That completely confuses me and makes me lose faith in you.
14. Don't tell me that my fears are silly. They are terribly real and you can do much to reassure me if you try to understand.
15. Don't ever suggest that you are perfect or infallible. It gives me too great a shock when I discover that you are neither.
16. Don't ever think that it is beneath your dignity to apologize to me. An honest apology makes me feel surprisingly warm toward you.
17. Don't forget I love experimenting. I couldn't get along without it, so please put up with it.

18. Don't forget how quickly I am growing up. It must be very difficult for you to keep pace with me, but please do try.
19. Don't forget that I can't thrive without lots of love and understanding, but I don't need to tell you, do I?
20. Please keep yourself fit and healthy. I need you.[31]

To this well-known memorandum I would like to add the following:

- Don't use force with me. It teaches me that power is all that counts. I will respond more readily to being led.
- Don't do things for me that I can do for myself. It makes me feel like a baby, and I may continue to put you in my service.
- Don't try to discuss my behavior in the heat of a conflict. For some reason, my hearing is not very good at this time and my cooperation is even worse. It is all right to take the action required, but let's not talk about it until later.
- Don't try to preach to me. You'd be surprised how well I know what's right and wrong.
- Don't tax my honesty too much. I am easily frightened into telling lies.

Many parents lead busy and complicated lives and cannot spend 24/7 with their children. However, we can learn to spend quality time with our children, recognizing that a Procrustean or one-size-fits-all approach will not work. You know your children, their strengths, weaknesses, trouble spots, and areas of excellence. Some children seem aligned with the gospel of Jesus Christ from an early age, while other children seem to question every tenet of Christianity and challenge every standard, boundary, and ethic of their parents.

Certainly some children require more time, prayer, consistency, structure, patience, meekness, and longsuffering. Your children will have many friends in their lifetime. If you have a choice between being their friend or being their parent, be a parent. Let them know what you believe. Let them know that you pray for them. Let them know what is appropriate and what is not appropriate. Set standards. Have family counsels and determine your family's principles and, yes, even rules. Some families develop a contract and have all family members sign the contract. They then post the contract in a place that is easily accessible. There is no way for the contract to cover all situations and possible scenarios because it is both behavioral and attitudinal. However, if the spirit of the family is incorporated into the contract, there will likely be greater unity, love, and family support.

Probably the most important piece of information I have ever given anyone is summarized in Doctrine and Covenants 121:39–44, where we find the Lord's guidelines for raising children, dealing with problems, and how to treat our spouses:

> *We have learned by sad experience that it is the nature and disposition of almost all men, as soon as they get a little authority, as they suppose, they will immediately begin to exercise unrighteous dominion. Hence many are called but few are chosen. No power or influence can or ought to be maintained by virtue of the priesthood, only by persuasion, by long-suffering, by gentleness and meekness, and by love unfeigned; By kindness, and pure knowledge, which shall greatly enlarge the soul without hypocrisy, and without guile —Reproving betimes with sharpness, when moved upon by the Holy Ghost; and then showing forth afterwards an increase of love toward him whom thou has reproved, lest he esteem thee to be his enemy; That he may know that thy faithfulness is stronger than the cords of death.*

As you probably know, this section of the Doctrine and Covenants was given in 1839. Some time ago I became very interested to find out if the definitions of the words from this section were the same back in 1839 as we find them to be today. I obtained a copy of the American Dictionary of The English Language (Noah Webster, 1828, First Edition) and looked up all the words I thought might have been different. Look at the following definitions and see if you are surprised, as I was, by any of them:

1. **Authority:** legal power; or a right to command or to act; as the authority of a prince over subjects, and of parents over children. Power; rule; sway.
2. **Power:** command; the right of governing, or actual government; dominion; rule; sway; authority.
3. **Influence:** in a general sense, influence denotes power

whose operation is invisible and known only by its effects, or a power whose cause and operation are unseen.

4. **Virtue:** in consequence; by the efficacy or authority.

5. **Priesthood:** the office or character of a priest. The order of men set apart for sacred offices; the order composed of priests.

6. **Persuasion:** the act of persuading; the act of influencing the mind by arguments or reasons offered, or by any thing that moves the mind or passions, or inclines the will to a determination.

7. **Long-suffering:** bearing injuries or provocation for a long time; patient; not easily provoked.

8. **Meekness:** softness of temper; mildness; gentleness; for-bearance under injuries and provocations.

9. **Unfeigned:** not counterfeit; not hypocritical; real; sincere.

10. **Hypocrisy:** simulation; a feigning to be what one is not; or dissimulation, a concealment of one's real character or motives.

11. **Guile:** craft; cunning; artifice; duplicity; deceit.

12. **Betimes:** soon; in a short time.

13. **Sharpness:** acuteness of intellects; the power of nice dis-cernment; quickness of understanding; ingenuity; as sharp-ness of wit or understanding.

14. **Reproved:** blamed; reprehended; convinced of a fault.

15. **Esteem:** estimation; opinion or judgment of merit or demerit.

16. **Enemy:** a foe; an adversary. One who hates or dislikes.

I hope these definitions can help you better understand what was expressed in the Doctrine and Covenants 121 when it was received in 1839. One of the many examples I have heard centers around the word sharpness. Here we see that in 1839 meant to be acuteness of intellect and understanding. The whole phrase, therefore, "reproving betimes with sharpness" takes on a different and more insightful meaning than perhaps we had understood before.

It is infinitely easier to destroy than it is to build. Our emotional bank accounts require time and many deposits to become established. While deposits require a great deal of care and effort, carelessness and casualness can cause withdrawals with not so much as a thought. A misspoken word, an irritable moment, a thoughtless action—and the withdrawals keep subtracting from our emotional balance and those of our children, spouses, friends, neighbors, acquaintances, and even strangers. The deposits, however, are not nearly so frivolously accumulated. They are built from persistent, consistent attitudes and behaviors.

There is a "hammer-to-a-nail" way of looking at things. If we see everybody around us as a nail and our only tool is a hammer, there is only one thing that can be done—a "one-size-fits-all" solution. One parent often will take an absolute consequence approach, while the other may be more soft, rescuing, and easily manipulated. We often see this in divorce or broken homes. The parents argue and fight, and the child's behaviors are ignored. This type of splitting will be discussed later. We must learn to find middle ground. The answer, of course, is balance.

The three C's of parenting teach us as parents and role models to ask ourselves:

- Did I cause it?
- Can I control it?
- Can I cure it?

We must accept responsibility for the things we have done wrong and teach our children and students to accept the responsibility when it is truly theirs.

A young, thirteen-year-old LDS boy was in a residential treatment center for youngsters whith psychiatric problems. His parents were principled but dogmatic, rigid, and unsafe. Home was helter-skelter and punitive with many orders barked out without principles backing them up. After three months of being in a psychiatric hospital, this young man was released. He put his arms around me and other people, weeping because he had never felt so happy as he had while in that unit. This is a sad commentary on his home life.

Some children who feel loved, protected, and secure in a psychiatric unit set themselves up so that they can come back. Confronting these children's parents often becomes difficult because they dictate their principles to you. Thus, right in principle—wrong in practice. Many parents seem to feel that they are right no matter what because they are the parents. However, it's not who is right but what is right.

We need to teach so that no one can misunderstand what we are saying, which is a much different approach than teaching so that others will understand. Sometimes we honestly believe, because we are throwing principles around, that we are teaching those principles. Instead we might really be making people defensive and upset. While we do not intend to be our child's enemy, we very often act like an enemy. The child makes a predictable conclusion, which in reality seems correct to them. They conclude:

- People who get after me are mean.
- My father (or mother) gets after me; therefore, he or she is mean.
- People who are mean don't love me.
- My mother (or father) is mean; therefore, she or he doesn't love me.

This may seem simplistic but, in reality, these are the very types of thoughts that children and teenagers accept as reality every day. Consider the next three spotlights:

1. "What's the use?" Dad shouted. "I'm always wrong! From now on you do all the disciplining. I'll just keep out of the way." Dad storms out of the room, leaving Mom bewildered and frightened. Their teenage daughter had just slammed her bedroom door after an ugly confrontation with Dad. She really had caused the family a lot of trouble by the choices she had made. So, why was it so wrong to point that out to her? How was she going to learn if someone didn't tell her?

2. A seventeen-year-old boy has a part-time job making approximately $500 per month. He comes to his mom and dad and announces that he has found a Camaro T-top car that is three years old, and he is absolutely in love with it and wants to buy it. Now, as parents, their first inclination was to "rain on his parade," which would have only made him angry; that is, their "natural man" or first reaction wanted to jump in and inform him how he would have to have full comprehensive and collision insurance and that the insurance alone would take as much as his car payments. They wanted to tell him that with interest on the car, he wouldn't even have enough money to drive the car, let alone insure it and make the interest payments. Had they followed their first impulses or their "natural man" reactions, the young man would only have gotten angry and felt that they were raining on his parade. It would have gotten stormy at

home. In this particular case, the parents handled it very well. Dad said, "I really like T-tops. That would be a lot of fun to have. I think it would be a good idea to check things out. Why don't you go down to the bank and check out what the payments would be and then call an insurance company and see how much the insurance would be to insure you in this car." Only a day later the young man came in; reality had rained on his parade but his parents were not the enemy. He had learned that the payments and insurance would have put him in the poorhouse and he would have had nothing. Again, it was reality and not his parents who gave him the reality check.

3.   A family, consisting of a husband, wife, and thirteen-year-old bright young man were seeing me one night for counseling. In parting, I said to the young man, "Your parents have an obligation to teach you correct principles. Ultimately, you must govern yourself and make those principles work." The young man looked at me and said, "What is a principle?" "That's going to be your topic next week. I want you to interview a few people and ask them what they think a principle is. Then you can look the word up in the dictionary. We'll address that next week." This was my closing comment, and as they left, Dad asked if he could talk to me alone for a few moments. He said, "Principles? You mean rules?" I knew the difference between principles and rules but I wanted him to learn it. If I just lectured him on the differences, it would only mean that I knew the differences; it wouldn't mean he knew. He ended up having the same assignment as his son, and we ended up working on it together.

"What is the difference?" you might be asking yourself. Let me help: Rules are imposed upon us and we may not have any emotional investment in them. When someone goes to prison, I have often heard others comment, "Well, didn't he know that was wrong?"

Knowing right and wrong is not enough for it to become a principle. Most of us understand the law, so to speak, but obeying the law or having some feeling about the law comes into what some have called the development of conscience, or being involved in the normative integration process of society. We are judged according to our light. Many young people understand right and wrong—that is, for example, that stealing is wrong—but they may still do that because they have not internalized this as a principle. Hence, the development of conscience. When sentencing is made at court, the person's age, knowledge, understanding, and experience are usually taken into consideration. Young people have, therefore, some amorality. Morality is something that develops, and we begin to have feelings about it. So, while the principles of the gospel are true, until the individual internalizes them and they become part of their conscience, normative structure, and set of principles, they do not have a built-in restraint system; it is only external.

Between external restraints and internal restraints, external restraints represent the one-way mirrors, floor-walkers, gadgets that set off alarm systems, and people checking your merchandise against your receipt as you leave the store. All of these are forces that lie outside of yourself and are external restraints or rule enforcers.

Internal restraints are a conscience, the Holy Ghost, values, ethics, beliefs, self-concept, and so forth. Ultimately, what really stops us from stealing are our internal restraints or principles. If external rules or restraints are the only things keeping you from stealing, you will eventually be in a position where you believe you can get away with it and you will attempt stealing. Simply put, it comes down to internal restraints or principles; they are what truly guide us. Thus, you have feelings about principles. They become integrated into your personality and become part of your core values and beliefs. But until those principles become your internal restraints, we may need to rely on the external restraints provided by and through the family.

This is one of the key reasons for establishing a family contract as was mentioned earlier. External rules can become internalized principles over time. It may sound simplistic, but once the children and parents have established curfews, made decisions about appropriate television or movie viewing, discussed and recorded decisions about skipping school or church, regulated views and decisions on important matters such as drinking and smoking, outlined appropriate respect and etiquette guidelines, and accepted the family's split on household chores, then, if and when problems arise with rules broken or affirmation needed to sustain the spirit of the contract, all you have to do is go back and review the contract. Everyone in the family has signed it. Everyone was involved in drawing up the contract. Now, if there needs to be a "heavy" clause, the contract is the "heavy" not the parents. It would be appropriate to review the principles, rules, standards, and guidelines of your contract every six months or so to keep the support of the whole family and learn important things about the family's current and changing views.

All family contracts will differ in length and specificity. In addition, everyone needs to understand that Mom and Dad aren't above the law. Some families itemize parts of the contract while other families, more in touch with what principles are, lean more on the spirit of the contract. These families may be able to include items like "Treat others the way you would want to be treated," "Do your chores with pride," "Be punctual to meetings and family gatherings," and "Be accountable for your own behavior."

Many people who think they are using good principles are, in fact, using rules to support them in their lack of patience, understanding, and inadequate parenting. They throw demands and commands out at their children with the firepower of an A-10 fighter jet. They quote scripture and verse where it gives them dominion and a sense of correctness. For instance, they may say:

- "Honor thy father and thy mother, that thy days may be long upon the land which the Lord thy God giveth thee" (Mosiah 13:20).
- "He that spareth his rod hateth his son: but he that loveth him chasteneth him betimes" (Proverbs 13:24).
- "Woe to the rebellious children, saith the Lord, that take counsel, but not of me; and that cover with a covering, but not of my spirit, that they may add sin to sin" (Isaiah 30:1).

As adults quote these scriptures, they ignore a critical principle: You can't expect more from children than you do from adults. What they really mean many times is, "Do as I say and not as I do." However, most of us know this never works very well for very long and most children as well as adults rebel under these circumstances.

Here are a few true principles that parents and other adults will often try to teach using incorrect teaching methods. While these are excellent principles, if we try to teach them with methods that include such things as beating someone verbally or physically, snarling, screaming, threatening, or name-calling, the respectful and pure parts of these messages will never come across:

- Don't you think that children should be honorable and honor their parents?
- Don't you think that cleanliness is important?
- Don't you think we should take care of our bodies?
- Don't you think that children should be cooperative and have responsibilities within the home?

- Don't you think that people should be thoughtful of others?
- Don't you think that children should respect adults?
- Don't you think children should learn responsibility?
- There is a right way to do a job and a wrong way. Don't you think that I have an obligation as a parent to teach them the correct way?
- Don't you think teaching gospel principles is important?
- Shouldn't we keep the Sabbath day holy?
- Shouldn't we always avoid any appearance of evil?

Going along with that list (which is not intended to be all-inclusive) is the following incident that explains how a parent can be right in principle and wrong in methodology.

My office is next to two psychiatric hospitals in Boise, Idaho. Some time ago a fourteen-year-old young man was in the hospital because of a suicide attempt and depression. He had been treated on an outpatient basis by a psychiatrist but had decompensated (a psychiatric term meaning "failure of defense mechanisms resulting in progressive personality disintegration") and had been admitted to the hospital. The young man had been in the hospital a couple of days and was stabilized.

During my first family meeting with him and his parents, I planned to talk about a few critical, life-threatening issues. As we sat down and began the family meeting, the father looked over and noticed that the young man had done some artistic work on the back of his hand. Dad immediately said, "I don't like the ink on the back of your hand. You could get blood poisoning. It also looks degrading and stupid." He continued, saying, "Your body is a temple, not a chalkboard. You shouldn't deface it."

This, of course, set the stage for our family therapy meeting, and we ended up dealing with issues like that rather than the reasons for the suicide attempt. Of course, I gathered a lot of information about how this family interacted, and I got to see first-hand how the father taught correct principles. I think this father rationalized what he was saying and doing because he was teaching "correct principles." Again, right in principle, wrong in practice.

We often use principles as an excuse for our own Trivial Pursuit games. You know what I mean, those conversations that focus on insignificant details with the underlying message or concern never coming out. A Trivial Pursuit conversation might go something like this:

Father: "I heard you come in after midnight last night."

Son: "It wasn't after midnight—it was before that."

Father: "Oh, what, 11:55?"

Son: "I don't know, but I know it was before midnight."

Do you think Dad was so uptight that he wouldn't be willing to forgive five minutes one way or the other? Of course not! What he may have been trying to say is "You were out pretty late and then you didn't check in. I didn't know where you were or what you were doing and I was worried." Now, this is a much different message than the one actually spoken!

Another example is this cartoon:

Notice the neighborhood children sitting on the ground, excited for the coming rain. To them, the approaching storm will be wonderful. But, to this man, the weather report triggered his "fight or flight" instincts. We may all hear the same lesson, the same talk, the same scripture, yet the information impacts each of us differently—and triggers different behaviors. Our interpretation of the information received is critical.

A man in his forties told me of the time when the happy, fun child died inside of him. He was approximately seven or eight years of age, and he was waiting for some expected company, including children who were about his age. He excitedly watched as the car carrying the visitors drove up the lane to his house. He ran out to his porch and was jumping up and down, yelling for happiness. His dad came up and slapped him on the head a couple of times and kicked him in the behind and said, "That's no way to act. You're acting like a blankety-blank idiot."

At that point, this little boy felt the happiness and joy drain out of him.

I feel bad for the lifelong sorrow this man has felt because of an error his father made. The following scripture may help him and others heal and move on:

> *For what glory is it, when ye be buffeted for your faults, ye shall take it patiently? but if, when ye do well, and suffer for it, yet take it patiently, this is acceptable with God.* (1 Peter 2:20)

Sometimes we identify a few areas in our life where we will have control. Perhaps we feel that the rest of our life is out of our control, and these few areas become our only way to maintain control in a chaotic world. We realize we cannot be perfect in all things, so we find a couple of things in which we can be perfect.

Monty, a man in his early sixties, came into my office, mainly because his wife insisted. He was incredibly angry and upset over his grandchildren constantly getting into his car with dirty feet or disturbing things in his garage. His garage, from what I understand, was something to behold. All of his tools were lined up in order with everything labeled.

Monty spent most of his weekends cleaning his cars and garage; in fact, he had little interaction with family and others on the weekends. A fitting epitaph on his headstone may read, "He really had a clean car and a clean garage."

Monty justified his behavior by pointing out correct principles. "Don't you think cleanliness and orderliness are important? Don't you think we should take pride in ownership?"

You can't ignore such principles. However, the practice of those principles to extremes had caused Monty to ignore more important aspects of life. I would certainly think that people would want something more important on their headstones than a line about cars and garages being clean. If the Lord came to your home and found a spirit of love and harmony, He would be pleased with your efforts—even if there was a load of laundry on the couch and strawberry jam on the counter.

> *In matters of style, swim with the current; in matters of principle, stand like a rock.*[32]

Chapter Five

BELIEVE THERE IS ONLY ONE RIGHT WAY TO DO THINGS

SO, WE REALIZE THAT OUR future, our destiny, and our eternal progression is up to us. We have prayed fervently and received the answer to pursue a particular course. Now that we have this insight, we are going to follow it to the letter. And, of course, as sane, rational, clear-thinking individuals, we realize that the truth is the truth; there can't be three ways to add up 3 + 2 = 5.

A loving Heavenly Father would not send multiple methods and ways of success down to his beloved children, would He? That would be confusing. It would mean that there might be more than one way to raise our children, or more than one appropriate way to support a family, or more than one righteous way to become successful. How could that work? Everyone knows there is only one right way to do anything! Right? Nope, wrong again!

Each of us comes to this earth with a unique perspective and a unique set of trials, abilities, and limitations. Psychology has identified an IQ or intelligence quotient to graph or rank how bright a person is. This IQ score is not fair, it is not impartial, and it is not our choice. However, it is the way it is. Many bright people have a difficult time understanding why things that are so very simple to them are not as simple to everyone else.

For instance, I have a teenage patient who is very gifted in math, science, writing, and memorization. He has a very difficult time understanding and building relationships within his own family because not all of his siblings are as gifted in these areas as he is. He feels that anyone who doesn't understand these things after a qualified teacher or tutor has explained them is either stupid or isn't trying.

Because of his perspective, he offends a lot of people. He has wrongly concluded that everyone has the same gifts, talents, and abilities. His perspective of reality is distorted. When I visited with him about the parable of the ten talents, he was annoyed because the servant who multiplied his two talents was rewarded the same as the servant who multiplied his five talents. "Shouldn't the one who multiplied five talents be further ahead?" he wondered. "Didn't he do more than the one who multiplied the two talents?"

No. Both servants magnified their talents equally, and both pleased the Lord because they did the most with what they were given.

> *If you are doing less than you can do . . . you are doing less than you should do.*[33]

Misunderstandings seem to be at the root of many common psychological problems. For example, many Christians wrongly think that consistently accomplishing a checklist of righteous activities constitutes righteousness. Many mothers strive to achieve "super momism." This attitude usually leads to an unhealthy emphasis on doing and less emphasis on being. When we operate in a checklist mentality, many items on our lists may be only cultural traditions and personal preferences, yet we view them to be as important as commandments.

Am I telling you that if your kids aren't in soccer, taking piano lessons, and learning a foreign language, you can still be considered a good mom? Do I mean that if you can't homeschool, drive to swimming lessons, teach a lesson on Sunday, keep a current family scrapbook, and fix a variety of meals during the week, you can still return to live with Heavenly Father? Yes! And, as Paul Harvey says, "Now for the rest of the story."

Feelings are not facts and thoughts are not truths. There is not just one way to do things. There is a difference between human preferences and practices and divine doctrine. Many of us have false expectations and actually contradict ourselves in our goals. Sometimes we do everything we feel or think is right and still our expectations seem foiled. Life is not just. "This is not fair," we say to ourselves. Some conclude that if I pay my tithing, "the windows of Heaven" will open and pour blessings upon me (see Malachi 3:10). However, the blessings may not be what we think or feel are great blessings or what we might have been expecting. Those blessings may come as lessons to be learned, knowledge to be gained, a new commitment to love. As we have discussed previously, it rains on the just and the unjust.

It is interesting to me that plastic surgeons are often sued by people who do not find life to be wonderful just because their ears stick out or their chin is a little bit different or their noses are nubbed off. Reality shows that those having cosmetic plastic surgery over and over are probably not really happy in life after the surgery either.

> *Your judgment and interpretation are only as good as your information.*[34]

Many of us forget that our emotions, feelings, and ideas may be erroneous. Because of the Fall of Adam, we are all vulnerable to things going wrong. We are not automatically entitled to correct information. Our physical, human, and carnal states have made us subject to frailties of mental, emotional, and physical dimensions. We are on this earth to subject the body to the will of the Spirit, but it isn't easy. Temptation is not the enemy; every person on this earth experiences temptation. Temptation simply means you are mortal. The enemy is succumbing to the temptations and either not recognizing our sin, error, or mistake or not repenting of it.

While none of us will achieve perfection in this life, we are expected to learn from our mistakes and from others' mistakes, and bring our defiant mortal bodies into subjection to the "enticings of the Holy Spirit" (Mosiah 3:19). We have to learn right from wrong and then choose to practice right instead of wrong.

Scientists have identified the emotional center of the brain, the limbic system, which exists in the lower part of our brains. The limbic system is near the pituitary and hypothalamus, both key components of the brain. The limbic system modulates a multitude of hormones, many of which function in ways scientists don't understand.

We do know, however, that the limbic system regulates things like glycogen from the liver, cortisol from the padrinal medulla, adrenalin from the adrenal glands as well as sexual hormones, sexual arousal, growth, sexual stimulation, feelings of excitement, feelings of love, and feelings of compassion. Interestingly enough, however, the limbic system does not differentiate between certain emotions. Excitement and anxiety both come from the same chemicals and areas of the brain. We determine whether we are happily excited or paralyzed with anxiety depending upon our definition and interpretation.

I've had people ask for tranquilizers because they were going to a ball game, movie, or rodeo in which they anticipated experiencing tremendous excitement. Most of us enjoy exciting activities. In fact, we often seek them out. However, we avoid anxiety. The physiological response to both of these is essentially the same; it is our differentiation of the response that counts.

We often experience feelings of passion, warmth, and goodness and it is up to us to determine whether these feelings are spiritually based or carnally or sexually based. Our brains cannot make the determination; we have to differentiate.

While feelings of passion and intimacy may be sexually based and perfectly appropriate when we feel them toward a spouse in a loving marital relationship, those same feelings conjured up for a counselor or church leader, if sexually based, would be inappropriate.

What other feelings arouse passion and intimacy? What about compassion, gratitude, and empathy? In a counseling setting, compassion, gratitude, and empathy would be appropriate, but not if they are misinterpreted as physical attachment or arousal, romance, and even love. Although the emotions may be the same, our interpretation of them is critical. Reality testing, then, is extremely important. We must ask ourselves where these feelings are coming from and if they are accurate, legitimate, and balanced.

One of the biggest, most ominous threats to the Church specifically and society in general is pornographic materials and the form of infidelity that comes from pornography and masturbation. Centuries ago, nudes were one of the major subjects for artists to paint. And, once photography arrived in the early 1860s, it didn't take long before a large percentage of photography was nude photography. Then, movie pictures came out. Not too long after that, we saw the move toward the use of movie pictures with pornography. As long as photographs were processed outside of people's own homes, the occurrence of pornography was somewhat controlled. Then came Polaroid and home videos, making nude photography that much easier. Now, we are facing a tremendous threat with the Internet. Most bishops have worked with ward members who have either become involved in illicit relationships through Internet chat rooms or struggle with pornography.

We have to ask ourselves, "What next?" What could be even more dangerous to the morality of our people? What development could be equally or more insidious? Are we sitting ducks for the next big evil—virtual reality? Is there a way to meet and face the challenge of pornography and Internet abuse within the Church before something like virtual reality enslaves us?

Virtual reality is not that far away. Even now, research indicates that people have stopped socializing. They find it easier to meet their sexual desires on the Internet without having to learn or exercise any social or people skills. They don't have to be nice; they don't have to be charming or have verbal skills; they don't need a sense of humor or civility. They can take care of their physical drive and be antisocial to boot. Imagine the threat of this to friendshipping, dating, and marriage—even to society in general. Virtual reality is probably only five to ten years away, and I suspect that what we have experienced from Internet pornography is only a drop in the bucket.

The divorce rate within the Church has increased. We need to challenge ourselves. Several excellent talks by Church leaders and other powerful literature dealing with these issues are available to help us combat these issues. With the expanse of information, let me mention two uncommonly good resources:

1. "Of Souls, Symbols, and Sacraments," a January 12, 1988, devotional address given by Jeffrey R. Holland, then president of Brigham Young University. In this talk, President Holland discussed with sensitivity the doctrinal seriousness of pornography and sexual relationships outside of marriage. He notes that if passion's flame remains unchecked or unrestrained, we are under the same condemnation that Alma described to his son Corianton when he said sexual transgression is:

> *An abomination in the sight of the Lord; yea, most abominable above all sins save it be the shedding of innocent blood or denying the Holy Ghost.* (Alma 39:5)

He also observed that sexual transgression is second only to murder on the Lord's list of life's most serious sins. (He noted that sins against the Holy Ghost were a special category unto themselves.) This is a wonderful talk and great resource.[35]

2.   "Personal Purity and Intimacy," a 1999 talk by Wendy Watson, a professor of marriage and family therapy in the School of Family Life at Brigham Young University. In her talk, Sister Watson tells us that "Satan's vision of physical intimacy is cunning, counterfeit, and contorting. Lucifer offers his skewed view of physical intimacy through movies, magazines, and music—actually through any and all publications and productions known to humankind—from stage plays to Internet chat rooms. When our vision clears and our frame is enlarged, we see the adversary's ploys for what they really are: elaborate and extensive maneuvering to capture our very souls. Lucifer covets your body and your spirit and those of your loved ones, and he is relentless in his sinister pursuit."[36]

The solicitation efforts that come over the Internet and even over cell phones are a temptation to all. While we continue to worry about our youth, as we should, we should also be concerned about the disruption and defilement of adults, as well as our families. The subtleties, the innuendoes, the covert imbedded messages are so alluring that the evil side is winning in large numbers.

'TWAS A SHEEP

'Twas a sheep not a lamb that strayed away
In the parable Jesus told,
A grown up sheep that had gone astray
From the ninety and nine in the fold.
Out on the hillside, out in the cold,
'Twas a sheep the Good Shepherd sought
And back to the flock, safe into the fold
'Twas a sheep the Good Shepherd brought.
And why for the sheep should we earnestly long
And as earnestly hope and pray?
Because there is danger if they go wrong
They will lead the lambs astray.
For the lambs will follow the sheep, you know,
Wherever the sheep may stray

When the sheep go wrong it will not be long
Til the lambs are as wrong as they.
And so with the sheep we earnestly plead
For the sake of the lambs today
If the lambs are lost, what a terrible cost
Some sheep will have to pay.[37]

I am constantly amazed to see the number of people who have been tempted, lured, and deceived, often by the manipulation of correct principles. They may say, "Don't you think people ought to have free agency?" "Don't you think that we ought to extend to others?" We must realize that the evil one is terribly powerful and incredibly subtle in his own way.

We all have heard the different variations that end this statement, "Too much of a good thing . . ." The pianist Liberace said that "too much of a good thing is wonderful." Excess seems to be popular to all generations of men. Many people believe we should follow this advice:

> *Eat, drink, and be merry, for tomorrow we die; and it shall be well with us. And there shall also be many which shall say: Eat, drink, and be merry; nevertheless, fear God—he will justify in committing a little sin; yea, lie a little, take the advantage of one because of his words, dig a pit for thy neighbor; there is no harm in this; and do all these things, for tomorrow we die; and if it so be that we are guilty, God will beat us with a few stripes, and at last we shall be saved in the kingdom of God."* (2 Nephi 28:7–8)

We all know what excess is and, simply put, too much of a good thing is still too much!

Dieting and exercise are perfect examples of too much of a good thing. When taken to the extreme and pursued with overzealousness, even these behaviors can be destructive. We've all seen people who are on low-carbohydrate diets and eat way too much protein. They lose weight but in the process throw their bodies off whack so much that they only have bowel movements once a week or so. We've also seen people who exercise to the point that they obtain that lean, hard body they are after, but they also experience shin splints or pulled muscles, or struggle with other physical challenges.

THE EXCESS EXPRESS

He worked out for years to reduce all his fat.
His muscles were firm and his stomach was flat.
He jogged nights and mornings to keep himself trim.
And still found some time to play tennis and swim.
He drank protein drinks, and ate health foods galore,
Then weight-lifted, cycled, and lifted some more.
He told wife and kids that it gave him a "high."
They said not a word, as he pecked them good-bye.
"If things work out right," he yelled back from afar,
"I'll make *Healthworld*'s cover! I'll be a big star!"
But, why could he not see the truck up ahead?
One thud—and his beautiful body lay dead.
And then he saw something that filled him with fright—
His spiritual body was one sorry sight!
A skeleton, covered with nothing but skin,
He got up to heaven . . . but didn't get in.
"Another soul's mine!" Satan started to scream,
"Give man something nice, and he'll take the extreme!
Okay, I'll admit it . . . I'll outright confess—
For the fast way to hell, take the Excess Express."[38]

In the New Testament we are told:

> *And ye shall know the truth, and the truth shall make you free.* (John 8:32)

Our physical bodies aren't the only things we sometimes take to extremes. There are many people in the gospel who develop pet projects or hobbies that all but consume them. They get completely out of balance as they do family history work, missionary work, or prepare their food storage. Sometimes they even neglect their spouses or children.

Heavenly Father wants us to be balanced. He wants us not to be over-zealous or "eager to the point of excess."[39]

Why do we become excessive? Why do we have a difficult time being balanced?

Society's skewed definition of what beauty is certainly contributes to the problem. On the covers of magazines and on billboards we see malnourished, even anorexic models, and our reality becomes what they seem to represent. Fat is not chic! And so, we get a mindset that if we don't look like these role models, not as these role models depict, something must be wrong with us.

In addition, many of us compare our fantasies to our realities. We compare our bodies and clothes with the bodies and clothes we can only dream of having. And we don't stop there—we often start comparing our real-life marriages and spouses with what we imagine others might have. Perhaps we have the concept of a slender, attractive wife who always dresses impeccably and looks terrific. Although we've only seen this dream wife in films, books, and advertisements, we still expect her to be real. We may even see someone who seems like her in real life, but we must remember we don't know enough about these situations to compare apples to apples, so we compare apples with oranges—an unfair comparison regardless of which you prefer.

When we compare, we always lose. As we make comparisons, our perception becomes critical. Even if we make what we consider to be honest comparisons, we often come out on the short side and so do our spouses, children, and careers. Most of us end up comparing our worst to someone else's best or our spouse's worst to the imaginary person we've created or with some other ideal. Comparisons are always detrimental.

The parable of the talents suggests strongly that Christ will judge people according to how well they have done, given their abilities and circumstances. Judging is a difficult task. Parents too often judge their children on their weaknesses, rather than on their strengths. "Why can't you play the piano as well as Don?" we ask Beth. "And, why aren't you as good at soccer as Tim or as good at writing as Jane?" Beth's self-esteem eventually hits rock bottom. While she might not write as well as Jane, she most likely does something better than any of the other children.

Ideally, we would resist the urge to compare. Most comparisons are conducted on such a haphazard basis that they're used simply to reinforce existing feelings of superiority or inferiority. Instead of comparing ourselves with others, we might profitably ask how well we are doing with what we have been given and how far we have progressed in the last week or month. We must answer these questions with an understanding of the principle of eternal progression, which says that we must constantly get better. In this life, perfection is a process, not a status. While we may become perfect in a few things, we will not become perfect in this lifetime.

Compare yourself to yourself only. If you must compare yourself with someone else, use at least thirty-five different criteria. You may not bake as well as Marge, but you may find out that in the thirty-five-criteria long-run, you come out okay!

If someone in your life seems to only identify your weaknesses or reminds you of all the things you aren't doing well, consider whether that person is one of the many or the few who thinks this. There will always be people who want to tear us down. The world could use more cheerleaders and fewer critics, but critics seem plentiful while cheerleaders are few and far between.

> *Great spirits have always found violent opposition from mediocrities. The latter cannot understand it when a man does not thoughtlessly submit to hereditary prejudices but honestly and courageously uses his intelligence.*[40]

I heard an old-timer say this:

> *It's not the ups and downs on the rollercoaster of life that bother us; it's the jerks in the middle!*

Amen!

Some people feel that at least one of the benefits of group therapy is that when we share our problems with others—and hear about theirs—we discover we wouldn't trade.

During one Relief Society lesson, the teacher asked each of the fifty or so sisters in the room to write down her biggest trial or problem in life. The sisters then folded up the papers and placed the papers in a basket. The basket was passed around, and each sister took out a piece of paper. "How many of you would rather have the trial that you wrote on your own piece of paper instead of the challenge that you have just drawn out of the basket?" the teacher asked. The vote was unanimous; every sister in that class chose her own challenge. Some of the sisters cried as they realized the magnitude of the trials other sisters were dealing with. Again, perception is everything!

I once counseled a man who managed a branch of a major bank. At the first of the year, when salary increases were given out, this man discovered that he had received only a 5 percent raise in salary. He had been expecting much more. Since he had taken over three years earlier, the branch had statistically far exceeded other branches, reporting fewer losses, better loans, and higher profit. He felt as though his good works had essentially gone unrecognized, and he was disappointed and angry. His perception of the situation was "nobody reads the statistical reports;

doing a good job doesn't count; and salaries must be prone to politics."

I told him that I couldn't tell whether his interpretation of the situation was correct because I didn't have the information necessary to make the judgment. However, I encouraged him to write down his thoughts, meet with one of the bank vice presidents and share his observations and interpretations in a tactful manner. I reminded this manager to follow the guidelines for effective problem solving: Use "I" messages, don't raise your voice, and so forth.

Although it took much courage, this gentleman took this advice and approached one of the vice presidents. During the interview, he learned that the bank had not done very well that year and, in fact, his 5 percent raise was higher than any other manager had received. Some of the other managers had even lost their company cars. When this man came out of the interview, his situation had not changed—he still would receive only a 5 percent raise—but his perception of reality, and thus his feelings, had changed dramatically. Although nothing had changed except his understanding of the facts, he no longer felt angry or unrewarded.

Chapter 6

ACCEPT ALL YOUR FEELINGS AS FACTS AND ALL YOUR THOUGHTS AS TRUTHS

OVER THE YEARS I HAVE had individuals come in and tell me they wanted a divorce from their spouses because they "weren't happy." As we talk, it often becomes clear that they aren't unhappy; they just aren't happy. In psychology, we refer to this as anhedonia.

Think about the difference between not being happy and being unhappy. If you are unhappy, you can usually pinpoint the reasons why. However, if you are just not happy, reasons for your feelings will be vague and difficult to identify.

One woman told me that her husband was a clerk in their ward and that they had to travel several miles to church. On Sundays, her husband had to stay after church for thirty to forty-five minutes. The woman waited for her husband. "It is awful waiting," she said. "I can't stand it. In fact, it's tormenting!"

Tormenting? I associate that with the word torture, where people pour acid down your nose, crush your knuckles, or put bamboo slivers under your fingernails. Waiting is not tormenting. It may be boring, even uncomfortable, but not tormenting. She could, of course, completely redefine the situation and see it in a positive light—as an opportunity to visit, for example. But even if she does choose to view the waiting in a negative sense, she should not over-dramatize the situation by using such an exaggerated term.

If we are in a situation that we feel is life threatening, our adrenaline system activates the body's "fight or flight" mechanism, a useful response if we have to defend ourselves or run for our lives. But a vocabulary built on death equivalencies makes less drastic problems seem much more severe. Whenever I hear people say something is terrible, horrible, catastrophic, or tormenting, I worry about them. Very few events in life warrant those extreme adjectives. How do these people respond when a real catastrophe occurs? How do these people manage the death of an immediate family member or another real tragedy?

One of the major differences between man and beast is man's ability to use symbols and language. Our language is like a program telling our computer-brain how to interpret the situation. If we tell our computer that something is horrible, it believes us and sends instructions to act appropriately. The brain doesn't know when we're joking, teasing, or exaggerating. Thus, we will overreact and cause ourselves unnecessary pain and trauma.

If, on a scale of one to ten (one being the worst and ten being the best), we only think in terms of ones and tens, our mind begins to fail us because the mind cannot handle ones and tens for an extended period of time. If we are genuinely in a one or ten situation, it is helpful to remember that these situations usually have two qualities: they are temporary and isolated.

As a professional, when I try to calm someone who is catastrophizing, exaggerating, or glorifying a situation, I begin by suggesting appropriate language. Whatever situation you face, try to describe it accurately. Make sure that you use adjectives and descriptions that are proportionate to the events at hand. If you are in the habit of using words in the one or ten category, consider adding additional words to your vocabulary. I've provided a list of words that are appropriate for each number on the scale:

1. Terrible, awful, devastating, catastrophic, tormenting, worst-that-could-happen, hell
2. Depressing, irritating, humiliating
3. Embarrassing, aggravating, upsetting, unnerving, painful, annoying, troublesome, gloomy, and uncomfortable
4. Boring, wearying, inconvenient, untimely

5. Ordinary, habitual, mediocre, routine, mundane, average, usual, everyday, common, okay, adequate
6. Above average, good, encouraging
7. Fun, reinforcing, enjoyable, rewarding, exciting, cheerful
8. Great, thrilling, stimulating, refreshing
9. Delightful, terrific, awesome, super, sensational, amazing, astounding, marvelous, exhilarating
10. Wonderful, glorious, fantastic, heavenly, celestial, once-in-a-lifetime

It would be silly to suggest that this relative scale or ranking is "correct" in some objective way. I use it simply to point out the rich possibilities for clear expression, expression that does not trap us in a circle of self-defeating thoughts but attempts to portray our lives as they really are.

We can easily talk ourselves out of forward progress or success with quite ordinary language. While the following comments contain very few words, the words are often exaggerated. These words can be powerful impediments to our efforts, which are key to success. Do you ever use or hear these common phrases?

- "That's going to be hard. I don't know if I can do it."
- "You don't understand how difficult this problem is."
- "But talking with him is so hard."
- "That would be scary."
- "It's easier said than done."
- "I can't do it!"
- "You're so dumb! How could you make such a stupid mistake?"
- "Oh, you're so fat; it's no wonder you don't have any dates!"
- "I'm so nervous; I'm going to make a hundred mistakes."
- "Oh, you're so ugly. No wonder all the kids hate you!"
- "Who'd date a three-hundred-pound woman?"
- "Who would want to go out with a guy who is broke and going bald?"

Do you sometimes fall for this kind of self-talk? Do you ever hear your children using these defeatist phrases?

Derogative self-talk needs to be tackled, even though sometimes it is ingrained in us almost as deeply as the color of our skin or the tone of our voice.

When we demonstrate a will not to succeed and then combine this with a vocabulary that thwarts us even more, we are simply setting plans for failure. But, if we can learn to pick up on these subtle messages to ourselves, we might yet succeed. Remember, the brain only knows what we tell it. If we persist in telling ourselves things that defeat us, we can only expect that our brain is going to work to make a reality out of what we have told it.

Not surprisingly, if we say things that make our situation more glorious or fantastic than it really is, our computer-brain will likewise be fooled. We may lose our composure and become less effective. Young people are often prone to exaggerated thinking. Suzy meets Johnny. He is wonderful, glorious, her soul mate, celestial—truly a godsend. Consequently, she can't do her math or English because her mind is focused on this fantastic boy she has just met. Then one day Suzy sees Johnny holding hands with Liz. This is a catastrophe! She can't stand it! Of course, she's immobilized again: she can't do her math; she can't do her English, and she becomes withdrawn and isolated. If this continues, a truly dangerous situation results.

"Can't" becomes a death equivalency because the only reason we cannot do something is that we are dead! When people say they cannot face this or that, their brain believes them and the people simply give up trying. If people say, "I find it uncomfortable dealing with myself" or "To take that class would upset me," then I can buy that. But "can't" usually leads to paralysis.

Another death equivalency that causes a significant amount of havoc in people's lives is the attitude that they have to have something. There is a major difference between wanting something and seeing it as an absolute necessity, essential for your survival. To "have to have" something rather than simply "wanting" it implies an emergency situation. This kind of thinking catapults us into negative circumstances. Some of the common notions that fall into this category are as follows:

- I must have everyone's approval, love, and respect.
- I must be intelligent, achieving, and effective in everything I do.
- I must have guarantees.
- I must have my own way.
- People must think and act the way I think they should.
- I must be in the know.

Wanting these things is not dangerous; in fact, wanting them is normal. The danger comes when we think having these things is an absolute necessity. Let's look at each of these separately:

I must have approval. We cannot get everybody to like us for everything that we do, and yet many people do try to please everyone. They become emotional chameleons and intellectual prostitutes. I often refer to this as the "tofu syndrome." Let me explain: What does tofu taste like? Well, tofu itself has no flavor. When combined with a chicken sauce, it tastes like chicken. When eaten with beef gravy, it tastes like beef gravy. In short, it tastes like whatever you put it with.

People with tofu syndrome appear to adhere to one value system and represent a certain set of thoughts and feelings—until their surroundings or their peers change; then they adapt values, thoughts, and feelings that seem appropriate in that setting. In other words, they placate others and discount their own values in a desperate attempt to get all people to like them.

In addition, these people make things very difficult for those who love them. Many times what they say turns out to be partial truths but they are fantasy-like or even fictitious. They brag or make up wonderful stories about how well they are doing. They know what people want to hear, and they know what makes them look good to those people, so they come up with wonderful stories about spiritual experiences, achievements, or opportunities that they are having. Some people do this to a point that they live in a fantasy land. Sometimes it can get more difficult because the mothers, fathers, spouses, and others want to believe in this person so badly that they actually develop a type of shared craziness—that is, they are caught up in the delusional or fantasy system that this person is making up.

When we make any kind of decision as an administrator, director, bishop, youth leader, elder's quorum president, Relief Society president, or parent, some people will be unhappy with our decisions. If we reverse or change our decision, we simply change dissatisfied populations on ourselves.

For example, if the bishop and Relief Society president decide to have a ward banquet for the whole family, some people will not like the decision because they feel that the function should only be for adults—a quiet private dinner to help the adults friendship each other. On the other hand, some of the people will be very happy with that decision, some won't care one way or the other, and still others won't come no matter what the decision is.

The very fact that many of us have chosen to be Latter-day Saints and Christians is an unpopular decision with some people. But if we spend our whole life trying to become what others want us to become and never really stand up for what we think, we eventually catapult ourselves into depression, realizing that we cannot have any stability in values.

I have to be intelligent, achieving, and efficient in everything I do. Another way to spell ultimate perfection in normal living is P-A-R-A-L-Y-S-I-S. If I felt I had to do everything perfect and could not stand failure of any kind, I would be immobilized. We can't do some things well. Certainly, we cannot do everything perfectly. Sometimes we just have to do it to the best of our ability. I think, too, it is important to realize that some things we can just do for fun. Perfectionists often heap devastatingly heavy expectations, not only upon themselves but upon their spouses, children, siblings, relatives, and church leaders. No one is ever good enough, fast enough, strong enough, smart enough, spiritual enough, or happy enough to meet the standard. The standard is elusive and can never be achieved anyway. However, if a person with perfectionistic tendencies sets realistic goals and accomplishes some and sees progress, he can sometimes gain some sense of satisfaction.

I must have absolute guarantees. While wanting guarantees is certainly understandable, when we have to have them, we stop most of the activities in our lives. We become paralyzed with fear. We must take risks in thinking and doing. Our society has become so success-oriented that we become fearful of trying.

Remember that failure can actually be a success if we learn new ways of thinking and doing. Certainly, no one actually ever became a great athlete without failing at some time. Albert Einstein said:

> *If we knew what it was we were doing, it would not be called research, would it?*[41]

I must have my own way. Many of us are so self-centered that we cannot stand to hear the word *no*. If we are thwarted in our activities, we throw a temper tantrum or we sulk. Mature people recognize the need for compromise in most day-to-day matters and strive to understand where their values allow for flexibility.

People must think and act the way I think they should. It's important to learn how to accept both defeat and compromise, which is either a partial defeat or a partial victory, depending on whether you see the glass as half empty or half full. Compromise is the way mature people deal with each other in our society. But neurotic thinkers who want to impose their will upon others often want to impose their mythologies about life as well.

> *When I was a child, I spake as a child, I understood as a child, I thought as a child: but when I became a man, I put away childish things.* (1 Corinthians 13:11)

Many people have not yet put away their childish things in this aspect of their lives.

I must be in the know. Some people believe that they must know all the details—all the good, bad, and indifferent—in everyone else's lives. They call and say, "How are you today?" When you respond, "I'm great!" they don't believe you. They may come right out and say, "Come on, nobody's life is great! Tell me what's really going on!" What a breeding ground for gossip!

These people seem to need the first, the latest, and the most sensational information, if not to pass on to others, at least to have the power of knowing what everyone else does not know. These people often talk more than others in a classroom situation, seeming to always need to disclose an important tidbit of information, a personal experience, or the details "as they understand them." Beware of such people! They may not hurt, deceive, or judge deliberately, but hurt, deceive, and judge they will do!

Many of us choose to run from our deeper feelings. People often come to me with ambivalent, contrary, or frightening feelings. They may be fixated on a number of issues, some of which need to be addressed and neutralized, some of which can be life threatening. If we deal only with superficial issues and fail to resolve the feelings that stem from deeper, unresolved issues of confused values or inadequate interpretive skills, we will never experience resolution. These feelings, however, can be exaggerated and compounded by the words that we use and by the way others treat us.

Elizabeth, a 22-year-old young lady who practiced bulimia to the extreme, looked essentially like a gutted whip snake. She was brought in to see me by her parents because they were gravely concerned about her health. Her potassium levels had dropped to a critically low state, endangering not only her health but also her life in general.

Through her tears, she told me how she believed that she was overweight. She would look into a mirror and see herself as obese, ugly, and unattractive.

This is an example, albeit an extreme example, of reality being one thing and interpretation being something completely different: No one else would define Elizabeth as obese or overweight, fat, or chubby. Yet, she alone maintained that concept of herself. If you were the only one who maintained a particular belief or viewpoint, perhaps it would be good to ask yourself, "Could I be wrong? Should I take a closer look at this?"

In order to deal with feelings, we must first be able to interpret them. One of the most important goals of mental health is to help people do reality testing, which is to determine whether what we are feeling is based on feelings or facts. As in Elizabeth's situation, some of us have feelings that may not make any sense to anyone else. In order to try to get down to where these self-images and impressions have come from, I ask them to fill out adjective lists for what I call the four different selves. Often, to make this easier I will give them a list of adjectives from which to choose or help them start the process:

- First, I have them fill out one adjective list, which they feel represents their *real self,* the person they perceive themselves to be.
- The next self is what I call the *ideal self,* the person that they would like to become.
- Next, I have them select the adjectives that depict the person that is the *feared self,* the person that they are afraid they would become.
- Fourth is the *presented self.* Many patients have a lot of difficulty with this self. This is how we believe others see us. We might call this the mask because it's the person we allow the world to see.

Sometimes to help them with the presented self, I ask them to get several people who know them to also fill out the checklist. Interestingly, most of the friends' evaluations are fairly consistent. Once all the checklists are completed on the different selves, we sit down and look at them. If the person is depressed, it's interesting to note that his real self, that is, the person that he sees himself as being, and the person that others describe are usually very different. Most of the adjectives under the real self are much more negative than the presented self.

RICHARD CORY

Whenever Richard Cory went down town,
We people on the pavement looked at him:
He was a gentleman from sole to crown,
Clean favored, and imperially slim.

And he was always quietly arrayed,
And he was always human when we talked;
But still he fluttered pulses when he said,
"Good morning," and he glittered when he walked.
And he was rich—yes, richer than a king—
And admirably schooled in every grace;
In fine, we thought that he was everything
To make us wish that we were in his place.
So on we worked, and waited for the light,
And went without the meat, and cursed the bread;
And Richard Cory, one calm summer night,
Went home and put a bullet through his head.[42]

Depressed people also have trouble discounting negative indications about themselves even if those indications are extremely isolated. We can't imagine a reason someone wouldn't like us because we try to like everyone else. To us, it seems incomprehensible that someone could simply choose to be mean, but that is the reality. No matter what we do, what we say, or what we look like, some people simply decide not to like us or to be mean to us.

Because we generally like and appreciate others, it is difficult to imagine that someone could simply choose to not like someone. It seems irrational, yet most of us have interacted with people who were mean or didn't like us.

Shortly after being called to serve as a bishop, I was warned that one particular woman would not like me. "Nothing personal," the former bishop warned. "She just finds fault with all leadership." Sure enough, within a few weeks, she made her move. Starting off with a few left-handed compliments, she said, "Bishop Nelson, I can't tell you how excited I am about the new things that are happening, blah, blah, blah. . . . However, I could not help but notice . . ." And then she went on to voice her concern that announcements were made in too much of a carefree style and that humor at the podium was probably not in the best interests of reverence.

I listened to her for a while and then smiled and said something like, "Your observations are certainly interesting, and I agree that it's probably going to be a difficult situation for you with me in the ward, and I really hope it doesn't bother you too badly." I let her know in a nice way that petty criticisms were not going to be taken very seriously.

After a few of these incidents, she left me alone, although, she continued to pick mercilessly on one of my counselors, who would spend hours listening to her recommendations on how the ward should be run. We don't have to allow these people to complicate our lives!

Many Latter-day Saints spend a lot of time saying things like, "I should," "I need to," "I ought to," "I have to," "I must." These are not encouraging thoughts. They seem to indicate that something or someone compels or commands us instead of allowing us to choose. These words also seem to imply that we are forced by a set of circumstances, rules, beliefs, traditions, or external pressures that disallow us to choose what we spend our time doing, that we are submitting to an unspoken set of boundaries that we actually may object to.

The Lord is not pleased with us when we force Him to compel or command us to do the right things. However, we can change the way we look at things and change our wording to reflect a positive way of thinking rather than a negative. If we replace the "I need to," "I've got to have," "I must" mentality with "I want to," "I choose to," "I'd like to," and "I will not," we automatically feel more hopeful, more powerful, and more in control. The "ought to" tasks that weigh us down become choices in a varied plethora of self-determining opportunities.

Doesn't it make you feel better when your thoughts don't beat you up? Why do we tend to always see the pits in our bowl of cherries? Why, after we have gotten all A's and one B, do we deride ourselves, thinking, "If I had only applied myself a little bit more, I could have gotten all A's"?

If your response to thoughts like these is a desire to try harder next time, then these thoughts actually can serve a purpose. In fact, they may even have their source in Heavenly Father. However, if these thoughts make you feel beaten down or depressed, consider the source of this guilt- and shame-based perfectionism. The Holy Ghost motivates us to become better; you won't feel beaten up after feeling His spirit. Conversely, Satan's methods will make you feel hopeless, helpless, frustrated, and devastated. Learning to discern between the two types of spirits is critical.

Defining and evaluating ourselves isn't always easy. However, as members of the Church, we have some special help in this quest—patriarchal blessings and other blessings often give us a glimpse of the way the Lord sees us, which is the only totally accurate perspective.

The Transactional Analysis of Ego States (hereafter referred to as TA) provides a framework for self-evaluation. It is a useful tool for cataloging and evaluating our behaviors and feelings and for understanding the dynamics of our interactions with others and with ourselves. TA focuses on the interplay of the different internal ways we have of looking at things, also referred to as ego-states.

The transactional approach to analysis says that there are different ego-states within each person and that we should try to establish a balance between them. Ego-states are not personalities but rather sets of feelings, emotions, assumptions, and conclusions. Each ego-state has different feelings and thoughts, and they are often conscious of one another.

The conflict between the different ego-states is real and can be intense. When people say things like "I feel like there is a battle going on inside me," it may well be that they are experiencing conflict between their different ego-states.

Knowing that people have different ego-states and that each person has different orientations, preferences, fears, values, beliefs, and even behaviors is very helpful. Most people are unaware that feelings may vary with ego-states. Often, after recognizing the discrepancy between the different feelings, a patient will ask me something like, "Is this how my wife (son, boss, or someone else) really feels about me?"

My typical reply is, "At this time and in her current ego-state, she probably does." This does not necessarily mean that a wife feels this way all the time—only in that ego-state at that time.

TRANSACTIONAL MODEL OF EGO STATES

Critical Parent — Fearful, cautious, speaks in absolutes, double-binding, always right in principle, critical, rigid, and negative

Nurturing Parent — Totally giving, loving, and nurturing

Rational Adult — Objective, rational, computer-like, unemotional, and practical

Spontaneous Child — Curious, irrational, fun, and spontaneous

Rebellious Child — Oppositional, stubborn, angry, and abusive

Adaptive Child — Pleasing, straight arrow, fearful, repressed, often depressed, perfectionistic, and double-bound

OUR INTEGRATED ADULT

To help us better understand these ego-states and their dynamics, it is important to look at the preceding model that identifies four key ego-states: the critical parent, the nurturing parent, the rational adult, and the child (spontaneous, rebellious, and adaptive).

The achievement of the integrated adult is our ultimate goal. That is, a logical, rational, objective adult integrated with the loving, caring, extending feelings of a nurturing parent and the fun and excitement of the free, spontaneous, curious child. I present this because I have always enjoyed this model to help us pigeonhole our emotions. This is called the transactional analysis model because a transaction is an exchange, verbal or nonverbal, between two or more persons or between two or more ego-states within your mind. All conversations between you and your spouse, you and your children, or you and yourself are a series of transactions, one exchange after another. Now, let's look at some of the characteristics of these ego-states. For the sake of clarity, I will refer to the ego-states as parent, child, and adult. Let's begin with the critical parent.

The parent in each of us likes to argue from principles. Since arguing from principles is considered an activity for the wise, the parent has the appearance of always being right. But being "right" can sometimes be both wrong and degrading to the child.

- The critical parent might say, "If you went to Sacrament meeting with a better spirit, you'd get more out of the meetings."
- "If you read the scriptures more consistently, you'd understand the gospel more fully."
- "If you did your genealogy work, you would better understand temple work."

All are true, but if your critical parent uses these truths as clubs to knock you down and beat you up, these comments become so overwhelming that you literally want to give up. Rather than being words of encouragement, they become demands that discourage and produce rebellion and discord.

The critical parent may also be double binding so that whatever you do is wrong. Let's use the example of seeing a professional counselor. The critical parent may say to the child in us, "Well, you've always been weak. You are the type of person who has always been dependent upon other people, and I guess weak people like you should see counselors."

Then, if you don't see a counselor but you truly need help, the critical parent may say, "Well, you always have been stubborn; you've never taken advice from people, and you always reject help."

Whatever choice you make, the critical parent inside may have a tendency to be highly critical and double binding. The critical parent may also make it impossible for you to accept praise of any kind. When you are stroked in any way, the critical parent inside may discount the praise. This, of course, has a great impact on interpersonal relationships because other people may tire of having their compliments discredited.

Conversely, in some cases the critical parent may harass the adaptive child, not into isolation but into dependency. This happens when there is constant criticism from the critical parent which leads the adaptive child to seek nurturing from others in an extreme, compulsive, or unhealthy way as a means of compensation.

However, if the nurturing parent in us can take over some of the nurturing, this dependency on others can be avoided. The nurturing parent is loving, kind, and accepting; it gives unconditional love. This may sound wonderful, but balance is essential because the overactive nurturing parent has a tendency to care for others at the expense of self. If your nurturing parent becomes dominant, then you will be easily exploited, and may wear yourself to a frazzle, yet still feel you can never do enough for other people. (This is undoubtedly one of the factors that contributes to codependency.) So, acting from the position of the nurturing parent without the balance of logic and reason from the rational adult becomes a personal weakness.

For instance, I know of one widow who spent her entire life's savings in legal battles to rescue her son from prison even though he was a confirmed criminal. This woman's nurturing parent was so much in control of her that she was unable to face reality and overcome her need to come to his rescue. The nurturing parent is typically pushed into the area of unhealthy excess by guilt and over-indulgence, which can, in turn, make children self-indulgent.

I recently saw an example of this when a mother found it necessary to admit her teenage son to the psychiatric ward of the hospital. Her son was completely out of control. He ran up and down the corridors of the ward calling his mother names and kicking doors. Although hospital staff members suggested the mother leave so they could calm her son down, she stayed, apologizing again and again to her son for admitting him. When the woman finally left, her son calmed down.

This mother was so consumed with guilt fed by her out-of-balance nurturing parent that she could not act rationally. Clearly then, there are dangers when the nurturing parent is not integrated with the logic of the rational adult.

On the other hand, if the critical parent becomes dominant, we may often hear critical parent messages such as "Negative feelings must be suppressed and forgotten," "The body and its functions are dirty," and "You should only think of others, not yourself."

Since the critical parent is so adept at making the adaptive child feel oppressed and inferior, many people want to attack the critical parent and eliminate it. However, this ego state serves a valuable purpose. We need to let the rational adult intervene as much as possible, without threatening the critical parent. The critical parent is like a mother bear in the woods. If we get between her and her cubs, she will tear us apart. Likewise, the critical parent, if threatened with annihilation, will attack ferociously.

Some therapists try to get the child or the adult ego-states to attack the critical parent ego-state by saying, "Get out of my life. I will have nothing to do with you!" While this may sound good on the surface, eventually the critical parent will return in stronger, more subtle ways.

Most parents realize no job is more overwhelming, or makes us feel more inadequate, than parenting. If we add to a parent's fear of inadequacy with threats, accusations, or alienation, that parent will usually retaliate—as does the parent ego-state.

When the critical parent is threatened, the correlating ego state sabotages all therapeutic efforts, whether those efforts are made by therapists or by the patient himself. To experience success, we must reassure the parent, by establishing and clarifying good values using solid reasoning and working out of a model of respect, that we accept the principles this critical parent believes. That part of the mind is actually important and, when given true and proper data, can be an important part of our conscience.

The critical parent does the best it can to keep us on the "right" path. Problems arise because much of the information we have fed into our critical parent computers are based on traditions, opinions, and personal preferences that may not fit our personal needs and may hinder our progress. Our rational adult, having the ability to reason this out and discard unhelpful beliefs, can assist the critical parent in its responsibilities.

However, the rational adult cannot assume those responsibilities by "getting rid of" the parent.

As indicated, there are three child ego-states:

First, there is the spontaneous child who is curious, irrational, and fun. This child in us would be the one to get an urge to go skinny-dipping and not consider for a moment whether you were with mixed company, whether you had a towel, whether it was 40 degrees outside, or whether it was approaching nightfall. This spontaneous child is innocent and precious but needs to be protected and reigned in by wiser, calmer, and more mature opinions.

Second is the adaptive child who cannot do enough to comply and continually tries to adapt to all wishes of the critical parent. This child in us continually, but passively, incorporates all of the problems, guilt, and frustrations of the critical parent. The adaptive child therefore placates by acknowledging and expressing guilt; but after the adaptive child has groveled in guilt long enough and the critical parent still does not let up, the adaptive child may become withdrawn, despairing, depressed, and even suicidal. Understanding this concept can give us further motivation to examine our beliefs and weed out unrealistic expectations, perfectionism, and other false beliefs that contribute to this depressing cycle.

Third is the rebellious child who crops up after the adaptive child has tried to please or placate the critical parent and failed. This rebellious period usually leads the critical parent to strongly reassert itself; renewed guilt is the predictable result. The cycle continues, of course, with more rebellion manifested in tantrums, passive-aggressive behaviors, conduct disorder, substance abuse, or suicide. The overt destructiveness of the final possibility—suicide—is symbolic of the destructiveness of the other stages of this kind of rebellion. Victories in these wars are purely pyrrhic, which means victory at any price, where really, everybody loses.

Any of these ego-states can be a problem if carried to extremes—we need to have balance made possible only through the integrated adult state. Below are some common issues that people have internal struggles over. Note the three columns and how the different egos states within us may affect our decision-making on each subject:

ISSUE: GOING TO A PSYCHOLOGIST, THERAPIST, or COUNSELOR

CRITICAL PARENT	ADAPTIVE OR REBELLIOUS CHILD	RATIONAL ADULT
You are sick and must see someone. You have always been weak and dependent. OR So now you won't go! You really are stubborn.	I'd better go and see someone; I'm so weak. OR Leave me alone! I hate the way you always try to make me the sick one!	Seeing a psychologist may help. I will see if my insurance covers this and check into the cost of competent professional help.

ISSUE: GOING TO CHURCH

CRITICAL PARENT	ADAPTIVE OR REBELLIOUS CHILD	RATIONAL ADULT
If you don't go to church, you will disappoint God and disgrace the family. OR God will not love you if you don't go. OR You better go so you don't have anything bad happen to you.	If I don't go, I will not get any privileges: no car, no friends, etc. OR You make me hate the Church. I will only hate it, and you can't make me like it.	A few hours a week is a small price to pay to have peace in my life. I choose to go to church.

ISSUE: TAKING MEDICATION

CRITICAL PARENT	ADAPTIVE OR REBELLIOUS CHILD	RATIONAL ADULT
Because you are weak and defective, you have to take medications. OR I don't know why you have to rely on medications. I guess you always have been weak.	I better take my medication because I am sick and weak. OR No one is going to poison me. You just want to control me!	It is practical to take medication—my doctor believes it best, and I am seeking his advice and opinion.

ISSUE: BUYING A CAR

CRITICAL PARENT	ADAPTIVE OR REBELLIOUS CHILD	RATIONAL ADULT
You want to buy a new car? Are you crazy? The payments, depreciation, and insurance will put you in the poor house. OR You're going to buy a used car? You really are dumb to buy someone else's headaches.	I really can't afford to make a mistake. What if I lose my job or choose the wrong car? OR I'll buy what I want. You have no right to tell me what to do.	I will weigh prices, insurance, financing, and warranties against my income and needs and then make the best decision I can.

This simple illustration uncovers the difference between the ego-states. The goal, as I see it, is to recognize that there is a purpose for all of these ego states within the balance of the personality. Without them, the rational adult ego-state is boring because it is void of feelings and emotions. The pure adult only looks at life in an objective, logical, rational way.

Granted, if all we had was the nurturing or the critical side of a parent, or the fun, free-spirited or rebellious side of a child with no logic and objectivity for balance, we would get into trouble quickly.

The goal has to be to minimize the negative dynamics between the critical parent and the rebellious child and temper and balance the self-sacrificing adaptive child and nurturing parent through the increased activity and involvement of the rational adult. The best outcome is an integrated adult with a little bit of the best of all sides.

Again, each of us has all of these ego-states within us all the time. That means that when we communicate with someone, they too have all of these ego-states within them. At any given time, your parent ego-state could be dealing with your spouse's adult ego-state, or one of your child ego-states could be dealing with your spouse's parent ego-state. Can you see how the ways in which we react to others become so critically important?

Although I'd like to think I can control which ego-state is doing the talking, I have moments when that integrated adult is fairly elusive. Sometimes, after a hectic day when I feel completely chewed up and swallowed, I like to spend some time alone when I first get home, so I retreat to my den.

Here's where I sometimes get into trouble. See if you can tell which ego-state is doing the talking here: My wife, Terry, knowing that I must have had a hard day, doesn't come to the door, doesn't say a word, and just lets me be alone. So after a few moments, I start thinking, "If she cared, she would come and see what's wrong!" That's my rebellious child talking.

But let's say Terry hears me go straight to my den. Realizing that I must have had a hard day, she comes to the door and says quietly, "Could I get you a sandwich or something to drink?" I burst out, "You know I sometimes just need to be alone! What's so difficult about that? Leave me alone!" This is my rebellious child ego spouting off again!

Perhaps you have similar examples in your own life and with your own spouse. Sometimes even the smartest among us are damned if we do and damned if we don't.

When I talk with patients about where their responses to certain situations are coming from, I approach them very carefully. A couple may want a loving relationship but repeatedly lock themselves in a war zone. A troubled marriage usually has too much covert communication, most of it outside of adult awareness.

One effective way to handle your differences is to negotiate them openly from your adult ego-states. With TA, you can examine your agendas, agreements, and contracts, both spoken and unspoken, and change them if you want to.

One of the problems in the way we think and react or respond dates back to the puritanical population that most of our northern European ancestors came from. Our founding fathers—Thomas Jefferson, Benjamin Franklin, George Washington and others—came from this same background. Hence, from the mouth of Benjamin Franklin we have quotations that show the upbringing, ethics, and high standards esteemed by those of that heritage. Some of Franklin's quotations may shed much light:

- A penny saved is a penny earned.
- After crosses and losses, men grow humbler and wiser.
- Experience keeps a dear school, but fools will learn in no other.
- Does thou love life? Then do not squander time; for that's the stuff life is made of.
- Work as if you were to live a hundred years; pray as if you were to die tomorrow.
- Well done is better than well said.
- Neither a borrower nor a lender be.
- When the well is dry, we know the value of water.
- He that hath a Trade, hath an Estate.
- Fear not death; for the sooner we die, the longer we will be immortal.[43]

Because of this puritanical background, traditional Christianity sometimes depicts God as merely tolerating man. God, therefore, becomes a witch-hunting deity that cannot wait to find out that we are not perfect so He can punish us. It is widely felt that the relationship you had with your parents as a child will affect the way you see God. It makes sense.

Many people have a difficult time picturing a loving, gentle, helpful, nurturing God, and based on scriptures in the Old Testament, that is understandable. We learn of God's wrath, God's fury, God's vengeance, and God's judgment, and then we wonder why we expect ourselves and others to be perfect! Let's see if we can change that.

Chapter Seven

STRIVE FOR IMMEDIATE AND ABSOLUTE PERFECTION

EVEN AS WE UNDERSTAND THAT there must be an opposition in all things, we must also understand that there is not truly a connection between something good happening now and something bad happening later. The bad things we experience don't happen because things are going well or because something good has happened in our lives.

There is some truth to the fact that after we experience a high of some sort, a natural letdown follows. For instance, we may head off for a long-awaited vacation with great anticipation and then return to reality and experience a bit of a low or lack of energy. This happens, and it is perfectly understandable. The problem occurs when we believe that because we experienced something enjoyable, we then have to be bored or discouraged. If this thinking was true, a causal relationship would exist. However, good does not bring bad; happiness does not bring sadness; sickness does not bring health; prosperity does not bring poverty.

Psychologists and ecclesiastical leaders commonly deal with people who hold on to guilt and are unable to move forward.

A woman once came to me who had been engaged in an adulterous situation many years previously. Although she had confessed to bishops, she also told me what an awful person she was and said she was confident that God could not love her. She continued about how she still felt black in her heart. As I realized that she had changed her behaviors and rectified the situation as best she could, I advised her to get on with living and let the guilt go, since it served no more useful purpose in her life. However, she told me that this was not true, that the ugliness (internalized guilt and shame) was going to remain with her forever.

Now, suppose her local bishop sends her to a regional leader or even to the president of the Church, and everyone she talked to tells her the exact same thing: forgive yourself and forget this problem. If she chooses not to follow this counsel, she has, in a very real way, preempted the government of the Church. She is basically saying, "I do not accept God's government in my life. Neither do I accept His love, forgiveness, and concern for me."

What value is there in hanging on to our sins? Do we misunderstand the Atonement so much that we refuse to acknowledge the wondrous gift of our Savior? Do we think we can or should somehow be able to pay for our own sins? Do we openly admit that we don't believe the Savior when He said He would pay the ultimate sacrifice for all of us and that if we but repent we would be able to take advantage of this gift? Is our thinking so grandiose that we misunderstand the purpose of our being on this earth in the first place? Guilt, to this extent, only serves neurotic purposes; nothing good can come of it.

Guilt can also be used to manipulate others—and even ourselves. I once evaluated a child molester who had been convicted repeatedly. When I introduced myself as the court-appointed evaluator, he immediately burst into tears. He told me what a terrible person he was to have done this to children. He said that he was not worth saving. His show of guilt was quite impressive, but the message he was really trying to send me was quite devious. At the same time he was telling me how awful he was, he was implying that he was really a good person because otherwise he wouldn't feel so awful. I can imagine him doing similar things to the judge, who occupies a parental role. And, if the judge listens only to the guilt and the tears, he may hear, "Please have mercy upon me because I am a good person; look how awful and terrible I feel" instead of "I am responsible for this."

Why is it so difficult for some to picture God as the ultimate parent—forgiving, extending, patient, and kind? Why do many of us profess to believe the gospel and support the leaders of the Church and then, regardless of counsel, choose to hang on to guilt, shame, failure, error, and the effects of sin rather than believe we can be forgiven?

In this latter day, we have the blessing of greater revelation and continued revelation through the leaders of the Church. We are taught the truth about the Atonement and about God's grace. Why, then, is it so very difficult to accept God's grace?

We've all heard of blind spots, and we touched briefly on them earlier in chapter 4. When people describe car accidents they've been in as the driver, it isn't unusual to hear the phrases, "I got blindsided" or "He was in my blind spot." Most people probably don't know where that popular phrase comes from.

We all have a little space in the back of our eyes where the optic nerve attaches. That space contains no nerves to pick up an image. Therefore, if the lens happens to focus the image right onto that space on the optic nerve, you will not see anything. You can test this by drawing two small dots, about the size of a pencil eraser, about four or five inches apart on a piece of paper. Hold the drawing in front of you, then close one eye. Look at the dot closest to your nose. Now pull the paper closer to your face, still focusing your eye on just only one dot. Look at your nose. All of a sudden, the outer dot disappears. The only thing you will see other than the dot on which you have been focusing is just the color of the paper.

I use that analogy because we all have blind spots—spiritually, mentally, and socially—and are naïve. Every one of us! Blind spots often create major problems for us and act as little traps in which we get ourselves caught.

It might help to try to picture the electrical circuit example from a few chapters ago. As long as there are no "breaks" in the circuit, the electric socket will function. However, if there is a break anywhere in the circuit, the electric socket cannot receive electricity. The break must be found and the circuit completed before the electricity is able to complete its function.

In the same manner, when we have unrecognized blind spots, these break the circuit and prevent appropriate behavior. Let me name a few of the most common social naivetés or blind spots that we each come in contact with every day:

- Exaggeration or embellishment
- Inappropriate laughter or loudness
- Interrupting others
- Poor hygiene
- Obsession with another's perceived weaknesses
- Biting fingernails or scratching scabs
- Intrusiveness
- Tardiness
- Flirtatiousness
- Sarcasm or cynicism

The list goes on and on. Certainly these social blind spots are often caused from spiritual or mental blind spots. The recognition of these areas within ourselves provides insight; however, correcting or preventing them requires judgment.

Some of the mental and spiritual blind spots would include:

- "Things are going well for me . . . knock on wood!" (in other words, happiness causes sadness)
- "I must be really bad for all these things to happen to me." (victim mentality)
- "Good things never last anyway, so why try?" (foretelling the future)
- "Our poverty, sadness, sickness or mental health is predestined by God and is the will of God. (We really don't have agency.)
- "Don't let the Evil Eye know that things are going too well because it will then cause them to go bad." (God merely tolerates man.)
- "If others knew the real me, they'd see how flawed and imperfect I am, and then they would never like me." (negative self-concepts)
- "I didn't make a mistake; I *am* a mistake." (shame or guilt-based indoctrination or control)

We often find children and teenagers from fine homes with these blind spots. It seems that a tendency toward perfectionism where the standards are set high often creates critical or shame-based guilt, as if we can't measure up. This appears to be the case even where excellent role models exist and in surroundings where guilt and shame were not used as motivators to control behavior. Some of us simply develop self-defeating behaviors and thoughts that constantly bring up the past and refuse to allow us to move on.

These feelings of negativism are deeply ingrained and result in a poor self-image with tendencies to discredit, devalue, and disparage ourselves.

Some people literally don't know how to behave in society. Perhaps they have grown up in hypercritical environments where implied guilt or fault existed no matter what they did. In such situations, people don't know how to fix their emotions. Should I feel guilty or ashamed? Is this my fault? Did I do something to cause this situation?

Certain social groups have appointed "judges." Judges exist in families, churches, school, employment, and in other social circles of our communities. The appointment of judges is critical because the assumptions we make about ourselves, regardless of what state we are in, are often inaccurate. We are all guilty of inappropriate behaviors and actions, but if the basic core of negative feelings that are shame-based are never resolved, maladaptive behaviors (addictions, anorexia, depression) continue.

During our formative years, when we are learning with little or no experience of our own, we need safe, non-shaming, benevolent significant others. This critical group often includes parents, grandparents, siblings, teachers, and church leaders. We need that validation through accurate empathy, an empathy that adds perspective to the person. In other words, we're looking for a positive significant other to help us build self-esteem, develop proper values, and make wise choices.

In multiple examples throughout the scriptures, we are told to repent, forgive ourselves, forget our sins, cease ruminating, brooding, or dwelling on the thing that was done wrong, and move on, praising God. Such was the case of the woman taken in adultery in the New Testament. Christ declared:

> *He that is without sin among you, let him first cast a stone at her.* (John 8:7)

Upon hearing this, the crowd departed. Jesus then asked:

> *Woman, where are those thine accusers? hath no man condemned thee? She said, No man, Lord. And Jesus said unto her, Neither do I condemn thee: go, and sin no more.*
> (John 8:10–11)

These reminders to repent and rejoice in the Lord are also found in the Book of Mormon. In one instance, Nephi is having quite a talk with himself:

Awake, my soul! No longer droop in sin. Rejoice, O my heart, and give place no more for the enemy of my soul. (2 Nephi 4:28)

Then two verses later, he reiterates these feelings:

Rejoice, O my heart, and cry unto the Lord, and say: O Lord, I will praise thee forever; yea my soul will rejoice in thee, my God, and the rock of my salvation. (2 Nephi 4:30)

The message in those two examples differs dramatically from the self-talk I hear so many times in my office. Self-talk is often full of expletives and expressions that define a person as bad, lazy, dumb, sinful, or stupid instead of appropriately identifying our behavior as being in error. With that negativism, we are subject to feelings of worthlessness and hopelessness that become part of our personality and identity rather than only occasional, temporary feelings.

One of the most common blind spots lies in the confusion between grace and works. The proponents of works present arguments and cite scripture regarding the necessity of works while the proponents of grace will do likewise with their point of view.

The blind spot occurs when we don't understand, refuse to accept, or deny the connection between grace and works. Both concepts are valid and important. The scriptures tell us:

For I the Lord cannot look upon sin with the least degree of allowance. (D&C 1:31)

The scriptures also declare:

Be ye therefore perfect, even as your Father which is in heaven is perfect. (Matthew 5:48)

Then, we also hear:

What, do you suppose that mercy can rob justice? I say unto you, Nay; not one whit. If so, God would case to be God. (Alma 42:25)

Many Latter-day Saints, as well as much of the rest of Christianity, have key principles mixed up or confused. We somehow believe that by enduring to the end and doing everything we can to be "good," we can in some measure qualify for God's kingdom through our actions.

For instance, let's say that you are honest in your dealings with your fellowmen; you believe in Christ; you obey the Ten Commandments inasmuch as you understand them; you have charity and compassion for your fellow inhabitants on this earth; and you do your best to be a good parent, a good son or daughter, a good sister or brother, and a good neighbor.

The difference between belief and faith is that faith requires action. Belief is a feeling; faith prompts us to demonstrate by our actions what our convictions are and how deep our conversion is to the gospel of our Lord, Jesus Christ.

All the good deeds mentioned above might be noteworthy and admirable. However, have you ever cheated on a test, stolen something from a store, been angry with your mother or father, been tempted by lust, gone shopping on Sunday, judged another person unrighteously, or wished that you had a Mercedes Benz like your neighbor?

Even if you have been a hardworking, honest person for twenty or fifty years, sometime in your life you have sinned. No matter how many years you remain "good" after that, you are fallen, damned, and imperfect. After that first sin in your own life, the only way you can hope to live with Heavenly Father again is through the Atonement. That's right— grace!

Our loving Heavenly Father knew that none of us could obtain perfection in this life. Therefore, He provided a plan whereby an ultimate sacrifice could be made, an innocent sacrifice that would pay for the sins of all.

Only One could fulfill that requirement—One who was innocent, who had never erred, and who loved us enough to take on all the sins, all the hurts, all the imperfections, and all the sorrow of every person, individually and severally, who had ever lived or who would ever live upon the earth. That person, of course, was Jesus Christ. He alone was able to take our shortcomings, our sins, and our deficiencies and make us whole. Whether you measure forty-five out of one hundred, twenty-three out of one-hundred, seventy-seven out of one-hundred, or ninety-eight out of one-hundred, only Jesus could take whatever we have to give and add the rest to make us one hundred percent perfect.

Many people believe that all men and women are created equal. I disagree. We are not equally talented or equally blessed. We don't have similar strengths or experience the same trials. We aren't able to relate to a one-size-fits-all pattern of success. Physiologic, hereditary, environmental, social, mental, and emotional differences seem to benefit some and put others at a disadvantage.

That is the wondrous thing about grace. To take advantage of grace, we have to acknowledge that Jesus is the Christ. We need to follow Alma's counsel:

> *Stand as witnesses of God at all time and in all things,*
> *and in all places that ye may be in, even until death.*
> (Mosiah 18:9)

Instead of our deeds earning us the reward of celestial life, our deeds, ideally, become what we do to thank a loving God and elder Brother for giving us the blessings of the Atonement.

We become better people because we understand this gift. We are humbled and grateful that the equation is Us + Christ = Salvation. At this point, we are accepted for salvation with certain conditions. If we endure to the end of our earthly struggle, whatever we have amassed in gifts, talents, and knowledge will be compounded to equal completeness, wholeness, and salvation. Are we perfect at this point? No. The journey to perfection continues after this life is over, but our Heavenly Father knows that we can obtain perfection eventually.

A loving, forgiving, compassionate, patient, and all-knowing Heavenly Father has given us the added blessing of the sacrament, knowing that none of us can proceed continuously without error. He has provided us with a way to regularly renew the covenants we've made with him, symbolically expressing our willingness and desire to stay on the path. He has also allowed us to recommit ourselves often with the hope of doing better and being forgiven over and over again.

> *For God hath not given us the spirit of fear; but of power,*
> *and of love, and of a sound mind.* (2 Timothy 1:7)

Now that we've explained grace and works, let's talk about the difficulty with striving for immediate and absolute perfection. Most of us strive for a successful life, whatever we may define that as, but we must understand that success does not come without payment. That is, we must learn to suffer, sacrifice, and put forth whatever it takes to accomplish what we desire.

In our quick-fix society, we want things immediately, and we don't want to pay very much for it. We often have false expectations and false ambitions. Perhaps we do have the physical and mental capabilities of "doing something." But maybe our batting average so far isn't impressive.

Most of us haven't created nor do we follow a life plan; we simply let life happen. Then, as we get older, we identify something we specifically desire, such as an education, a deeper knowledge of the scriptures, or a certain career. Sometimes these desires cause us to make certain decisions and take certain actions so we can achieve our desires. However, while many of us may desire specific things, we don't have the slightest idea how to obtain those things, nor are we willing to do what it takes if we did know.

We mistakenly expect that perfection, significant worldly goals, and accomplishments can be attained by simply asking. I believe that even manna from heaven had to be prepared in some way before it was eaten, and certainly not very many people make it big in the lottery mentality of life.

Spencer W. Kimball wrote a book called *Faith Precedes the Miracle.* Why didn't he call it *Belief Precedes the Miracle*? Faith is an active word. Belief is not. Faith takes effort. Things don't happen by sitting around waiting for the lottery to occur. Even Cinderella, as lovely and nice as she was, didn't do much on her own except be nice. Had it not been for her fairy godmother, she would still be sitting around weeping in the ashes by the fireplace and getting nowhere.

Faith indicates that we must act for ourselves and get up and move.

It has been said, "If you are waiting for your ship to come in, you better have sent one out."

I often ask patients, "Which is the easiest to control—our thoughts, feelings, or behaviors?" What do you think? While our thoughts and feelings may fluctuate greatly from day to day, we do have the power to control our behaviors.

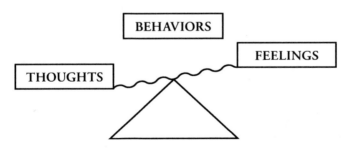

Our thoughts and feelings—whether high or low, good or bad, noble or base, and everything in between—may be subject to a great many complex variables. The easiest then, and the area I suggest that we challenge the most, is our *behaviors*, and not focus on the feelings and thoughts.

For example, we already know some of the things that depressed people think and feel. There are probably many reasons a person might not want to get out of bed; depression is just one of them. Let's imagine that a person has his knees operated on and has been sitting in a wheelchair for six months. The doctor tells him, "It is time you got up, put some weight on those knees, exercised, and got about doing some more activities." The person responds, "When I do not feel awkward or clumsy and my pain stops, I'll do that." That person will probably never get up from the wheelchair. The behaviors are the emphasis, not what the person might feel or think. He will have to push past what he is thinking and feeling in order to rehabilitate from that knee surgery. The important thing here is a person's behaviors—his actions. The same holds true in mental health. Let's look at depression only from a behavioral standpoint. What does a non-depressed person do? A non-depressed person will do the following:

- Act as if he is not depressed.
- Arise and get cleaned up and dressed at a reasonable time each day.
- Take time to set goals for the day and have a plan for doing them.
- Be active, smile, volunteer, and attend events of interest.
- Do many good things of his own free will.

William James, a nineteenth century philosopher, developed this idea and called it the "As If" principle. The philosophy behind the principle says that if you want to be brave, act as if you are brave. If you want to be righteous, do the things that a righteous person would do. If you want to be patient, act as if you have great patience. It is a little bit like telling the truth in advance. Whatever characteristics you wish you had, act as if you already have them. This can be phenomenally successful!

What does a depressed person do every day? His behaviors are many times opposite from the non-depressed person and are quite predictable:

- A person who is depressed usually behaves depressed.
- If he gets up in the morning, he stays in his pajamas late into the day, acting like a couch potato.
- He will not go out and socialize.

- He shows low energy, lethargy, fatigue, withdrawal, social isolation, and alienation.
- He spends the day eating and lounging around the house, and many times doesn't answer the phone. Day after day may pass in the same fashion.

I would suggest that someone struggling with depression might think about getting up fairly early and be dressed by a reasonable time every day. He may want to try setting daily goals and even establish a plan for accomplishing those goals. He should be as active as possible. The very act of being active will often bounce us out of a situational depression and offer us a more accurate interpretation of our circumstances. After working with hundreds of seriously depressed people, I have come up with one sentence that instills the recipe for success:

Marshall your efforts to change your behavior.

Another type or series of events in our lives that can distort our reality is taking on a perfectionistic notion. Much of this tendency started when we were very young and had heard many of the following statements. While they may sound encouraging, they are also very self-limiting. Only one of these phrases has any scriptural basis whatsoever. Have you ever heard any of the following "proverbs"?

- Anything worth doing is worth doing well.
- If you can't do it right, don't do it at all.
- Time is money.
- Idleness is the devil's workshop.
- Waste not, want not.
- Idle hands make for mischief.
- Rolling stones gather no moss.
- A watched pot never boils.
- You are what you eat.
- If it's to be, it's up to me.
- If you want something done right, do it yourself.
- If you can't say something nice, don't say anything at all.
- Don't bite the hand that feeds you.
- Children are to be seen and not heard.
- It's easier to do things right than it is to do them over.

- It's my way or the highway.
- Don't put all your eggs in one basket.
- Use it up; wear it out; make it do; or do without.
- Unto whom much is given much is required.
- If there's a will, there's a way.
- You can do anything if you set your mind to it.

Let's just work with only the very first one: "Anything worth doing is worth doing well." When I was thirty years old, I thought I had had this instilled in me, and I came close to dying just because of some stress and overwork. I changed that personal commandment in my life to this:

Some things are worth doing well.
Some things not worth doing are not worth doing well.
Some things are just worth doing for fun.
Some times you just get by.

Let me use an example: What if you got up in the morning and you knew company was coming and you said, "I have to have my house cleaned up" and, of course, "anything worth doing is worth doing well." But there is no way you could do it well. So, then, based on that proverb, you shouldn't do it at all. Right? No, not right.

Okay now, let's take one more, the last one. It says, "You can do anything if you set your mind to it." I hate to be the bearer of bad news, but you really can't do "anything" if you set your mind to it. Am I being a pessimist? No, no . . . hear me out. At my age I cannot really become a professional football player; that is not going to happen no matter how much I set my mind to it. One more example: I have absolutely no art or spatial ability. I marvel at people who can look at a person's face and draw a good representation of that face or even a cartoon version of that face with seemingly little effort. That will never be my ability or talent.

I can have talents in other areas. I need to experiment with different things and find out where my talents are. Sometimes, however, people chase rainbows. Spending six years in college to become an engineer and ending up with a barely passing grade won't do a lot of good while job searching. Even though you may graduate, employers are looking for those at the top of the class, not at the bottom.

A man can fail many times, but he is not a failure until he begins to blame someone else.[44]

Out of this entire list, only one of these phrases is scriptural, yet several of these may well have affected our thinking and our emotional responses to life as deeply as if they were commandments. Remember that perfection can be spelled P-A-R-A-L-Y-S-I-S. What if we can't be perfect?

Remember that we've been programmed since we were children. When this programming took place, we were naïve. We lacked experience and had little or no background to be able to reject or accept these notions.

> *For all have not every gift given unto them; for there are many gifts, and to every man is given a gift by the Spirit of God.* (D&C 46:11)

Recognizing our strengths and weaknesses can be a real eye-opener. In almost everything we do, we will face people who like what we do, those who won't like what we do, and those who don't care either way. Our Father in Heaven expects us to be solid like the

> *Wise man who built his house upon a rock.* (3 Nephi 14:24)

However, some of us resemble the wind, blowing to and fro, back and forth, making decisions by mere whimsy. Some of us don't show any foundation or reinforcement whatsoever, like the

> *Foolish man, who built his house upon the sand.* (3 Nephi 14:26)

One of the best things about Christianity is the foundation it provides that can identify each believer as Christian. Certainly, there are differing practices, doctrines, and identifying behaviors, but the underlying foundation—that we believe in Jesus Christ—remains the same. This all culminates with the Golden Rule and, generally speaking, civility.

We have talked in this chapter about striving for perfection and the paralysis it may cause. We've talked about the "As If" principle and how it can help pull us out of dark times.

However, Satan still has some very powerful tools in his arsenal, tools that he is able to get many to actually volunteer to use against themselves with no more than a little urging.

Just one of these tools or weapons creates amazing distortion. After we use it effectively on ourselves, we are then more expert to use it against those we should otherwise value, trust, and protect. But the consequences are huge! Why, this one tool can destroy relationships, ostracize friends and neighbors, and alienate brothers and sisters. It enables Satan to take pieces of truth and twist them around until our attitudes are distorted and vague. The distortion is a little like a woman looking in a mirror of warped glass at a carnival fun house and trying to put on lipstick; she's going to end up a real mess! We will discover this tool in the next chapter.

Chapter Eight

ALWAYS DISCOUNT, DISCREDIT, AND DEVALUE YOURSELF AND OTHERS

WE'VE TALKED A LOT ABOUT different weapons in Satan's arsenal. So which one is the most damaging, the one that destroys us and our relationships the most?

Negative self-talk. Through negative self-talk, we convince ourselves that the things we say about ourselves are true. Remember what we learned earlier about the brain? It doesn't know when we are joking, exaggerating, fantasizing, daydreaming, lying, or telling the truth. It simply accepts everything as truth. Knowing this, we can make a few assumptions, including the following: "If I can make myself feel worse, I can make myself feel better." "If I can increase my pain, I can decrease my pain." "If I can increase my anxiety, I can decrease my anxiety." "If I can increase my fear, I can decrease my fear." Through appropriate self-talk, we can change our outlook of "have to's," "musts," "need to's," "can'ts," and "shoulds" to better reflect the truth about our situation.

How important would you say it is that a rodeo rider project a positive outcome about each ride that he takes on a bull or bronco? I think it's safe to assume that if we asked the country's best bull rider what he says to himself just before a ride, he wouldn't say, "Well, you know, I never fully expect to ride that bull for eight seconds. I expect to be bucked off immediately, and I just concentrate on not getting kicked in the head as I sail toward the ground."

Of course, a champion in any event would have better self-talk than that! But what about self-talk for the rest of us, those who might not hit any grand slams, who might not make any three-point baskets during overtime, who might not shoot three under par even once in a lifetime— you know, you and me?

We are the producers of our own thoughts, yet we are also the victims of our own thinking. How does this happen? We can start answering that question by asking another one. Does charity conflict with humility? Not at all! Look at the Savior when he began his mission. He went to a synagogue and, as was the custom, stood in front of the group and opened the scriptures. He knew who He was and what He had to do. A more humble man has never lived on the face of the earth. But He did not hide who He was.

As He stood there in front of those people that day, He knew the stir of anger that was about to be created as He read in the scriptures about a coming Messiah. He then declared,

> *Today this scripture is fulfilled in your ears.* (Luke 4:21)

No wonder the Pharisees were offended by His words! Wasn't He approaching arrogance? Of course not!

You and I are not the Savior, Jesus Christ, and we have no business comparing ourselves with Him. Christ counseled us to

> *Love thy neighbour as thyself.* (James 2:8; see also D&C 59:6)

This seems reasonable as an abstract idea. However, in the mental health field, we often find people who have no appreciation for themselves. If they don't appreciate themselves, how can they appreciate a neighbor, brother, sister, friend, or stranger?

People sometimes despise and are cruel or even punitive to themselves. These people have a genuinely difficult time extending kindness, charity, or love to others. It's hard to esteem other people if you have no esteem for yourself. If we despise ourselves we will disguise our true selves, never letting others know our inner beauty. We can never have intimacy and closeness with other people until we begin to love ourselves. We cannot extend kindness and charity to others until we care about ourselves?

Many people feel that there is something sinful or bad about loving themselves. Others confuse self-esteem with lack of humility. Some people have found that if they discount or discredit themselves, other people will jump in and bolster them up. They say things like, "Gosh, that was stupid! How could I have done that?" To this remark, a caring companion or friend might say, "Don't beat yourself up like that. It wasn't your fault." Individuals who fall into this pattern often are seeking attention or looking to escape responsibility.

Other people walk around in sackcloth and throw ashes over themselves in an effort to show humility and seek penance for their many unreported sins. This behavior comes from growing up with a particular extreme indoctrination.

The negative self-talk I am describing occurs with people who have either grown up in a devaluating home environment or suffer from serious depression and, consequently, have no regard for themselves. These people see themselves in a negative light. They feel and act subservient. They feel and act unattractive. They feel and act as if they could never measure up. They feel and act as if their opinions are worthless.

In extreme circumstances, some have so much guilt and shame, or have accepted so much blame, that they make attempts on their lives or engage in self-inflicted violence (cutting, hitting, burning, scratching).

Often, because they feel that their opinions are worthless, they are unable to set boundaries for themselves and others. A boundary is a limit or edge that defines you, and most of us have limits to what is psychologically and physically safe for us. We have—or should have—emotional, spiritual, sexual, relationship, intellectual, and physical boundaries.

Emotional boundaries define our self, ideas, feelings, and values. We set emotional boundaries by choosing how we will allow people to treat us. Our spiritual boundaries are developed from our inner self and sense of who we are; only we know the spiritual path for ourselves. We have sexual boundaries, limits on what is safe and appropriate conduct. Our intellectual boundaries offer us the opportunity to enjoy learning and teaching, allowing us to be curious and inspired.

Because many of us grew up with unhealthy boundaries, we often normalize hurtful behavior and can't recognize boundary distortion.

The following are types of boundary violations:

EMOTIONAL VIOLATION

1. We deny our feelings.
2. We are told what we can and cannot feel.
3. We allow ourselves to be screamed at.
4. We are belittled.
5. We have a lack of expectation.
6. We are terrorized or threatened.

SPIRITUAL VIOLATION

1. We go against our personal values to please others.
2. We believe in a hurtful or vengeful higher power.
3. We have no spiritual guidance.
4. We have no sense of prayer or gratitude.

SEXUAL VIOLATION

1. We are sexual for others, not for ourselves.
2. We seek or allow the wrong type of attention to fill the void in our hearts.
3. We were denied sexual information during puberty.
4. We were given misinformation about our bodies.
5. We feel ashamed for being the "wrong" sex.
6. We are exposed to pornography.
7. We are subject so sexualized comments.
8. We are victims of any forms of sexual abuse.

RELATIONSHIP VIOLATION

1. We fall in love with anyone who reaches out to us.
2. We allow others to take as much as they can from us.
3. We believe that others define our reality.
4. We believe others can anticipate our needs.

INTELLECTUAL VIOLATION

1. We are denied information.
2. We are not allowed to make mistakes.
3. We are not encouraged to question.
4. We are called stupid, retard, moron, etc.
5. We are encouraged to follow a parent's dream.
6. We are told how to think or feel.

PHYSICAL VIOLATION

1. We accept touching that we don't want.
2. We are not taught appropriate hygiene.

3. We are victims of violence, excessive tickling, or hitting.
4. We are deprived of touch.

Before we can establish healthy boundaries, we must identify boundary violations in our own lives. Think about significant people in your growing-up years, and write their names on a list. Reflect on the six areas of boundaries as you consider each person. Distinguish those who observed or taught you healthy boundaries by putting a "1" by their names. Note "2" next to the names of those with whom unhealthy boundaries were experienced.

Numerous blinking or neon lights should come on when a person sees, feels, experiences, or identifies a number of unhealthy boundary violations.

The following is a list of common signs of unhealthy boundaries; however, this list is not meant to be exhaustive or all-inclusive.

SIGNS OF UNHEALTHY BOUNDARIES
- Telling all
- Talking at an intimate level at the first meeting
- Not noticing when someone invades our boundaries
- Not noticing when someone else displays inappropriate boundaries
- Touching another person without asking
- Allowing someone to take as much as they want from you
- Letting others direct your life
- Letting others define your reality
- Believing others can anticipate your needs
- Accepting food, gifts, touch, or sex that you don't want
- Being sexual for your partner, not yourself
- Falling in love with a new acquaintance
- Being overwhelmed or preoccupied by/with another person
- Going against personal values or rights to please others
- Expecting others to fill your needs automatically
- Falling apart so someone will take care of you
- Believing your feelings, strengths, values, beliefs, don't count
- Being responsible for the feelings of others
- Physical and sexual abuse. Sometimes we don't have boundaries in these areas and at times we may be abusing others or we may be allowing others to abuse us

The norm of reciprocity is an important term to understand because it helps us recognize when something has gone wrong with our boundaries. For instance, let's imagine a sixteen-year-old young woman starts dating an eighteen-year-old young man. Within a very short time, she has told him that she loves him and has shared every intimate secret imaginable. The young man feels uneasy about this. His new friend has exchanged information that is not reciprocal of the information he has exchanged. He is private and modest about his body and is uncomfortable with the amount and extent of information that she so easily discloses.

Relationships have to be mutual; they are a give-and-take situation. The reciprocity doesn't have to be in identical ways. For example, a worker who produces a certain amount of work doesn't ask for work in return but gets, instead, a certain amount of money for his labor. As long as it remains fairly balanced and reciprocal, this system is okay. However, some people try to buy friends, position, or influence and eventually some expectations are made; at this point the system becomes out of balance. I am confident that many of us have felt uncomfortable asking ourselves, "What does he want from me?" or "What is he really after?" Having a well-balanced and mature boundary system is critical to getting along in any relationship or association whether it be marriage, work, or friendship.

A favor today may become a duty tomorrow.

In my work through relaxation or imagery techniques, I try to get certain critical self-worth/self-esteem-type messages into people's heads. I often tape these sessions, and I have them listen to them at different times. While all of these sessions turn out to be their own unique experience, the basic messages are similar:

"I am John or Jane Doe, and I am unique and different. In all the billions of combinations of variables in the world, there is no one else like me. There may be a few people who have some parts like mine, but in the long run, no one adds up exactly like me. Therefore, I realize that everything that comes out of me is unique and authentic; it has rarity and exceptionality. Most important is the fact that I own me.

"I own my eyes, including all the memories they see. I own my ears, including all the sounds and words they hear. I own my feelings, whatever they may be—whether joy, love, anger, or excitement. I own my behaviors, whether they are toward me or toward others. I own my triumphs and successes. As I go through this life, I will find out some things I do not know about myself, but I will not find out many more things. However, as long as I choose to be friendly and accepting toward myself, I can find the courage to look at these things and make whatever changes are necessary.

"However I look and sound, whatever I say and do, whatever I think or feel at any moment in time is me. When I review later how I looked and sounded, what I thought or did, I may decide that this is not right for me. But because I own me, I have the power to change or discard those things that are not right or good for me. Further, I can replace them with new and creative ways of being. That which I have proven right and good, I can keep.

"As owner, I am engineer and architect of my own life. I realize the importance of free agency and the power of choice. When God gave me the freedom of choice, He also gave the promise that if I use my freedom of choice with justice and creativity, I will be productive.

"Not only can I survive, I can make a difference! Perfection is a process, just as life itself is. And as I begin to understand this, I enjoy the journey more."

Former South African President Nelson Mandela used the following during his 1994 inaugural address. The original author, Marianne Williamson, is a well-known author and speaker on spiritualism.

> Our deepest fear is not that we are inadequate. Our deepest fear is that we are powerful beyond measure. It is our light, not our darkness, that most frightens us. We ask ourselves, who am I to be brilliant, gorgeous, talented, and fabulous? Actually, who are you not to be? You are a Child of God. Your playing small doesn't serve the world. There's nothing enlightened about shrinking so that other people won't feel insecure around you. We were born to make manifest the glory of God that is within us. It's not just in some of us—it's in everyone! And, as we let our own light shine, we unconsciously give other people permission to do the same. As we are liberated from our own fear, our presence automatically liberates other [45]

The message in "The Touch of the Master's Hand" makes me weep each time I read it. Although some may feel it is referred to too often, I feel it has a place here:

THE TOUCH OF THE MASTER'S HAND

'Twas battered and scarred, and the auctioneer
Thought it scarcely worth his while
To waste much time on the old violin,
But held it up with a smile:
"What am I bidden, good folks," he cried,
"Who'll start the bidding for me?"
"A dollar, a dollar"; then "Two! Only two?"
"Two dollars and who'll make it three?"
"Three dollars once, three dollars, twice;
Going for three"—But no,
From the room, far back, a gray-haired man
Came forward and picked up the bow;
Then, wiping the dust from the old violin,
And tightening the loose strings,
He played a melody pure and sweet
As a caroling angel sings.
The music ceased, and the auctioneer,
With a voice that was quiet and low,
Said: "What am I bid for the old violin?"
And he held it up with the bow.
"A thousand dollars, and who'll make it two?
Two thousand! And who'll make it three?
Three thousand, once, three thousand, twice,
And going, and gone," said he.
The people cheered, but some of them cried,
"We don't quite understand
What changed its worth?" Swift came the reply;
"The touch of the master's hand."
And many a man with life out of tune,
And battered and scarred with sin,
Is auctioned cheap to the thoughtless crowd,
Much like the old violin.
A "mess of pottage," a glass of wine;
A game—and he travels on.
He's "going" once, and "going" twice,
He's "going" and almost "gone."

But the Master comes, and the foolish crowd
Never can quite understand
The worth of a soul and the change that's wrought
By the touch of the Master's hand.[46]

A Church member once shared a discussion she had experienced with her bishop. The two knew each other well, and as they sat together for a temple recommend interview, the bishop found an opportunity to teach a principle. He asked her as they began, "Do you want the easy interview or the difficult one?"

The member, not knowing what to expect, said, "Let's try the easy one first." The bishop then proceeded with the standard interview, reviewing the commandments and the member's general worthiness.

As they concluded, the member's curiosity got the best of her and she asked what the hard interview consisted of. The bishop said, "I'll tell you what the questions are, but rather than trying to answer them now, think about them between now and our next interview." The bishop then outlined a list of questions:

- When did you last help your neighbor?
- When did you last do so anonymously?
- When did you last help your enemy?
- When was the last time you did good to those who you knew hated you?
- How long has it been since you blessed those who curse you?
- Which Christ-like qualities have you added to your character in the past year?
- When was the last time you engaged in earnest, private prayer for 15 minutes or more?
- In what specific ways have you improved your relationship with your spouse during the last year?
- What are the most memorable one-on-one experiences you've had with each of your children recently?
- Whom have you forgiven lately?
- How often is the priesthood used in your home?
- Do you hold any grudges?
- Whom do you think you are better than?
- How do you prepare for worship in Sacrament meeting each Sunday?

- What charitable acts have you done during the past month for people less fortunate than you?

As my friend left the bishop's office, the bishop had a parting comment: "Remember," he observed, "even the rich young ruler who met Christ passed the easy interview" (see Mark 10:17–25).

Each of us can learn something from this story. We often believe that if someone has more, then someone else has less. We have the competitions between the Joneses to see who earns the most money, who has the best kids, who serves in the best callings, and even who is the best neighbor.

Unfortunately, in a setting of competition, an air of contention often appears. Although Heavenly Father would like us to be happy when others succeed, rather than feeling that their success somehow takes away from our success, our natural-man response often dictates our feelings.

We can find many examples of this, but I especially like this one from Harold S. Kushner's book, *When Bad Things Happen to Good People*:

> *One time, there were two haberdashers (merchants) who had stores across the street from one another and had, over the years, become bitter competitors. They would spend a great deal of time standing in the doorway tending one another's businesses. When one would get a customer, he would smile in triumph at the other one and take the new client inside. Their rivalry and anger grew unchecked for many years. One night, an angel appeared to one of the men in a dream. The angel said, "God has sent me here to teach you a very great lesson. God will grant you whatever you wish, but you must understand that whatever you are granted, your competitor across the street will be given twice as much. Would you be rich? You may be richer than a king, but he will be richer. Would you have children that you may be proud of and that are famous? You may, but his children will be more famous. Would you live a long and healthy life? You may, but his life will be longer and more healthy. The man frowned and pondered for a considerable time. Finally he told the angel that he wished to be struck blind in one eye.*[47]

None of us want to admit that we want others to fail. Yet we have a tendency to judge others and ourselves by the yardstick of the success of others.

> *Ye have heard that it hath been said, An eye for an eye, and a tooth for a tooth: But I say unto you, That ye resist not evil: but whosoever shall smite thee on thy right cheek, turn to him the other also. And if any man will sue thee at the law, and take away thy coat, let him have thy cloke also. And whosoever shall compel thee to go a mile, go with him twain. Give to him that asketh thee, and from him that would borrow of thee turn not thou away. Ye have heard that it hath been said, Thou shalt love they neighbour, and hate thine enemy. But I say unto you, Love your enemies, bless them that curse you, do good to them that hate you, and pray for them which despitefully use you, and persecute you; that ye may be the children of your Father which is in heaven: for he maketh his sun to rise on the evil and on the good, and sendeth rain on the just and on the unjust.*
> (Matthew 5:38-45)

When I was on my mission, my companion and I began teaching a man who was severely alcoholic. He was a bachelor who often holed up in his dirty apartment. By teaching him the gospel, we showed him some new options in life. He was baptized right before I was transferred to another city. Six months later, I returned to the city where this man lived.

When I met him again, I didn't recognize him until he threw his arms around me and embraced me. The familiar physical symptoms of alcoholism had disappeared, and he was cheerful and surrounded by friends. He had chosen an entirely new lifestyle. The change occurred through his own efforts and the gospel of Jesus Christ. All we as missionaries had done was present an alternative way of life that he had not been aware of. He had done the rest with God's intervention because his desire for change was great enough.

In teaching correct principles, it goes without saying that we hope those we are trying to teach will understand what we are saying. Speaking in tongues was a common miracle in early Church history and, in fact, continues to be a wonderful experience today. If you've ever seen this happen, you may find it uncomfortable to witness people speaking in a foreign language. However, most of us speak in a foreign language quite a bit and don't even realize it!

As Latter-day Saints, we often speak of Relief Society, the priesthood, Primary, the Doctrine and Covenants, the Pearl of Great Price, garments, stake meetings, and so forth, presuming that others understand us. Sometimes we speak in acronyms such as LDS and MIA. We have used these acronyms for so long that we may not even know exactly what they stand for.

Likewise, military personnel often say someone is going TDY. If you ask them what TDY stands for, they often don't even know. The definition, found on a government Web site states: "TDY stands for 'temporary duty yonder.' It is defined as duty at a location(s) other than the permanent duty station."[48]

We find numerous examples in the computer industry, which uses all sorts of acronyms and presumes that everyone knows and understands what they stand for. Examples include RAM, ROM, CD, and CPU. These are just a few examples that illustrate the importance of clear communication.

We also use acronyms in psychology, often talking about OCD (obsessive compulsive disorder) and OCP (obsessive compulsive personality), and ADD (attention deficit disorder). I sometimes tease people and tell them that they are O-D-D, meaning odd, nothing more!

People with OCP are commonly found in religious settings. Obsessive compulsive personality is not obsessive compulsive disorder. It is a personality type and not a disorder. The difference is that individuals dealing with OCP are often highly principled people. They have worked certain ideas out in their minds, and they quote principle after principle to support their views; they become right by definition. These people store many principles in their heads. Sometimes people will even take scriptures out of context and use those scriptures to justify their principles and their obsessive compulsive natures.

As we communicate, we may use words like chaste, virtuous, moral, honest, integrity, and straightforward. Because we see the people being taught nodding their heads up and down like bobble-head dolls, we presume that they understand.

Unfortunately, admitting that we don't understand what another person is saying can be embarrassing or intimidating. We worry that the person who is talking might think we aren't smart enough or we aren't worth the effort. We worry that we might be laughed at or make people angry with us or be belittled for our lack of understanding.

Isn't it better to go with the flow? Shouldn't we just laugh with the crowd or pretend we understand? Shouldn't we just keep up the bobble-head bounce in our church classes?

No! If we want to succeed at something, we have to apply correct success principles. And, just like in all other areas of life, success principles exist for correct, clear communication. If we want clear, untainted results, we must give clear, untainted directions.

A young woman newly married stayed home one Sunday from Church, anxious to prepare the Sunday meal for her in-laws. She explained that she was going to cook a roast and make baked potatoes, and because she hadn't learned a lot of domestic skills, she asked if there were any instructions or anything she should know. Trying to give her new daughter-in-law the simplest advice possible, the mother-in-law replied, "The only trick to getting the potatoes done in one hour is to poke each potato with the end of a fork before baking them."

When the family arrived home several hours later, the new daughter-in-law began setting the table and there, sticking out of the ends of each potato, were forks! When asked what this was all about, the young woman said, "Well, you told me to poke each end of the potatoes with a fork before baking in order for them to be done in one hour." The instructions that seemed so clear, so simple, and so unmistakable had turned out to be anything but clear, simple, and unmistakable to this young woman.

I like the following little cartoon:

I would be interested to hear what the original instructions were for this little guy. Obviously, he can plant teddy bears all day long and he's never going to get one to grow. Likewise, in communication, if we don't understand the principles to make our communication effective, we might as well be planting teddy bears!

Good communication is often based on good principles. The instructions given in Doctrine and Covenants 121 offer excellent guidance. Earlier in chapter 4, I defined many of these more unfamiliar words with the help of the American Dictionary of the English Language. I have used section 121 of the Doctrine and Covenants with many people not of the LDS faith, and many of them found it rather profound, particularly when we use the correct definitions. As was mentioned a little earlier, sometimes we use words like chaste, moral, virtue, and integrity but don't know what they mean. In addition to understanding what our words or someone else's words mean, there is a way to problem-solve correctly based on communication principles. Although they seem fairly simple with my background, I know that these skills are not as commonplace as I might wish they were. Therefore, I offer my guidelines to communication and problem-solving and will offer comments along the way where clarification may be necessary.

GUIDELINES FOR
COMMUNICATION AND PROBLEM SOLVING

• **There is no right or wrong to feelings.** There is right and wrong to actions, of course, but feelings, no. It is interesting to hear how people justify their behaviors by their feelings. For example, "I hit him because he made me mad." All of us have told children that two wrongs do not make a right. Yet, as adults, we often apply the same logic as we commit similar errors

• **Don't tell another person how he feels. Ask.** People do not like their minds read. When you tell someone how he thinks and feels, you are usually going to get back a negative reaction.

• **Provide feedback. Repeat back. Paraphrase.** Mirror or repeat back what people say, and then work up to a point where you can paraphrase. This is an interesting art that takes patience but doesn't take very much time. Paraphrasing is repeating back significant words that people say to you. For example, if a child says, "I think it is really cool" and you say, "You think it is really awesome?" you may have a fight. "I didn't say awesome," the child might reply. "I said cool."

Once a young girl came to see me. As we talked, she used numerous superlatives and swear words. Of course, I didn't repeat back all of the words, especially the superlatives. Instead, I used empathetic listening to mirror her.

"I really hate my blankety-blank-blank-blank family," she said. "All they blankety-blank-blank-blank do is yell and scream, yell and scream. That's all they do is yell and scream and, then, blankety-blank, they say, I am flippant and sarcastic, and I don't say one blankety-blank word!"

"So, you really hate your parents," I reflected back to her. "All they do is scream and yell. They say you are flippant and sarcastic, and you don't say a word." Then I proceeded to ask her a few more questions that I hoped might initiate more communication. "Tell me more about that. Help me understand that. Can you explain that a little further?"

"That's right, all they do is scream and yell." she said.

I said, "All they do is scream and yell?"

And she said, "Well, they get loud."

"They get loud," I said, "Tell me more about that and help me understand."

"Well, like I said, they get loud. But what really makes me mad is they say I'm flippant and sarcastic, and I don't say one word."

"You don't say one word?"

"Well, I don't say it verbally. But when I roll my eyes and flare my nose that sets them off."

"When you roll your eyes and flare your nose that sets them off. Is there more? Can you help me understand this?"

She finally said, rather calmly, "No, that's all." Finally, she felt that at least she had been heard.

Now at this point, paraphrasing is appropriate. We paraphrase to make sure that we understand what happened. So in this instance, I said, "Your parents get loud and when you roll your eyes and flare your nose that seems to set them off." At this point we now have something we can talk about. That's workable. Her opening phrase was not workable.

• **Deal with feelings first, facts second; it's okay to disagree about facts, but feelings need to be understood.** I watch people often get lost in details. For example, you might hear these kinds of dialogues:

"You drink too much."

"Maybe I have a beer or two once in a while."

"You drink four or five or six beers sometimes."
"One or two."
"Five or six."
"One or two."
"Five or six."

The actual number is irrelevant. The feelings are what are important here. In this instance, the feelings behind the words might be "drinking scares me" or "drinking brings back old memories of when I was a child and things were out of control."

Another dialogue might be:

"You were an hour and a half late last night."
"I was an hour and fifteen minutes late."
"An hour and a half."
"An hour and fifteen minutes."
"An hour and a half."
"An hour and fifteen minutes."

The facts are not important, the feelings are. This person might be trying to say, "When people don't let me know they are going to be late, I worry, and it scares me." Those are the feelings—and the most important fact behind this communication.

• **Don't stockpile or gunnysack feelings. Deal with problems within twelve hours.** Many who do this work in a pressure-cooker model. Eventually, the frustration and anger comes out, and it can come out in an ugly way when we stuff it. Yes, we have been told in the Church to watch for teaching moments and those teaching moments are not usually at two o'clock in the morning when people are angry and upset or drunk. But we do need to revisit the problem.

• **Take time out if you feel you are losing control, and then come back to the original subject.** Just as in ball games, sometimes timeouts are necessary. Timeouts play a critical role in allowing us to collect our thoughts; they allow us to recognize that we might lose control and say things that aren't good. We must allow others to take timeouts as well. Following behind someone as they walk away, yelling, "No, we're going to talk about it now! We're going to talk about it right now!" This accomplishes nothing. You may talk about it right now but it may be ugly.

• **Know and respect each others' sensitivities.** We all have sensitivities to certain words, jokes, behaviors, humors, and gestures. It amazes me when we get angry how we quickly forget those sensitivities and go for the throat. When you do that, you may win a pyrrhic victory. That is, you may have won the argument, but the cost was so high that it may have caused you to lose the relationship.

• **Use "I" messages, not "you" messages.** Avoid the accusatory "you" messages, the finger pointing, the "you must" or "you have to" messages. These messages create defensiveness. I had a patient who, while talking about her problems, began whining and sounded like a World War II air siren. She started low, but as she became more involved, her voice would rise to a high-pitched, ear-piercing whine. If it was bothering me, I could only imagine what it was doing to her husband!

My natural inclination was to fire a bunch of "you" and "your" accusatory messages at her: "You are simply driving me crazy. Your whining is ear piercing. If you are driving me mad, you have to be driving your husband to drink!"

Instead I said, "As a psychologist, I have been in numerous years of training and gone to hundreds of hours of workshops to learn how to communicate. But sometimes I get lost in a conversation. I often look like a little doll with my head nodding and appear to be paying attention when actually I am not; I have dissociated. That means I can be fishing or hunting or working on my cabin in my head but look like I am paying attention. When people raise and lower their voices, I am especially distracted." She caught the message and did fairly well for an entire half-hour before going into her whine. As soon as she did that, I simply said, "Excuse me, but I noticed I started to get distracted."

• **Never blame.** Don't use shame or blame in communications. These are "you" messages and they only fire off defensiveness.

• **No physical or verbal threat or abuses. Avoid high volume voices or screaming.** Again, your principle might be right, but yelling, screaming, and threatening are poor teaching methods. Even if people look like they are listening to you, when they feel threatened, messages simply don't get through.

• **No sarcasm and/or barbs.** These only turn people off and they stop listening to what you are saying.

• **Deal with one subject at a time.** Don't eat the elephant all at once. Don't try to solve every problem at once.

- **Don't use the past to punish. Use it only for reference.** We all have pasts. Sometimes we have to talk about the past as a reference, but when we use it as a way to punish and abuse people, it only prevents effective communication.
- **Avoid all-inclusive words including never, always, every time, and without exception.** These are often part of the "you" messages that we know we should avoid. Still, we sometimes say things like, "You never take me out." "You are always leaving your stuff out."

First, "you" messages create defensiveness and often cause people to argue or fight with you. Second, they are seldom the truth. Nobody does anything all the time.

- **Avoid critical parent communications, such as "should not," "have to," "ought to," "should," and "must."** These words and messages only create more anger. Again, they,are "you" messages. Nobody, including a child, likes to be talked down to.
- **No interrupting.** This is rude and disrespectful, and only makes others resent whatever you are saying or teaching.
- **No emotional blackmail.** Let's say you take a three-year-old into a grocery store and he asks for a candy bar. "It's too close to dinner," you say, "and I won't buy you a candy bar and not buy one for everyone else."

He says in his mind, "I'm going to get the candy bar and I'm going to do so by embarrassing Mom." He throws himself down on the ground, bangs his head on the ground, and starts screaming that he wants a candy bar. If you give him that candy bar, you are in big trouble next time you take him to the store.

So, as we grow up, how do we use blackmail and terrorism to get our way? The silent treatment comes to mind. Other approaches include the "cold shoulder treatment," "I'm going to get angry and throw myself about," "I'm going to get a divorce," "I'm going to walk out," "I'm going to punch holes in the walls," and, of course, the ultimate is "I'm going to kill myself!" This emotional terrorism is not much more sophisticated than a three-year-old throwing himself down on the grocery store floor, kicking and screaming.

- **No emotional double-binding.** In a double-bind, no one wins; both parties lose. A couple came in once with the wife bitterly complaining that her husband "never" did anything fun, frivolous, or romantic. When I had him alone I suggested that he try doing something fun, frivolous, or romantic. He agreed, and that week he bought his wife a wildflower bouquet mix in a vase and left it on her desk at work with a cute love note.

When she came home, she was furious. She'd been teased at work, and all he'd been trying to do is what she said she wanted. Neither person won in that instance. Double binds are difficult to understand and take a lot of adult courage to unravel. For instance, what if your child tells you her grades are bad. You're probably furious. However, if she had lied about her grades, that would have made you angry too! Again, a double bind.

Double binds must be looked at openly and correctly. The thing that you have to ask if something bothers or upsets you is, "If I flip the coin over, will the opposite behavior also bother me?" If it will, you are in a double bind.

Perhaps someone tells you that you have bad breath or you are not performing well at work or your paper wasn't good because it did not have this quality or that quality. Those realities may hurt, but what if those people did not feel brave enough to make those criticisms or give you those comments? Certainly, these become possibilities for double binds.

• **No lecturing.** Lecturing is a poor way to teach correct principles. If I lecture you on a topic, all that means is that I claim to understand the topic. It doesn't mean that you have learned it. Many lectures, of course, turn to "you" messages and are blaming.

• **No name calling.** This seems to be a given. It is low-class and profane and only sets up anger and defensiveness.

• **No hidden agendas.** When you have something vital to talk about, make an appointment to talk and talk in a place where you will not be disturbed. Schedule a couples meeting or a family meeting, and have an agenda. I have met many couples and families who discuss issue upon issue but never resolve anything.

If every time I saw my wife I got a stomachache and every time she saw me she got a headache because we were bringing up certain issues that never got resolved, I would eventually start to avoid or ignore her. I suggest people get a notebook and leave it in a particular place and write agenda items down. Once a week, they discuss agenda items. Some items will be on the agenda for a considerable period of time before being resolved, while others can be resolved quickly.

Typically, these items are not fun to talk about, but the problem comes when they continually appear and are never resolved; then they begin to erode relationships.

• **Do not argue principles.** Principles are always correct to the person holding them. They make sense, and they can't be argued. However, sometimes people use their own principles to beat up on others and justify their positions. For instance, let's take a look at all-inclusive words and fighting with principles.

Jane says to her husband, George, "You (accusatory) never (all-inclusive) take me out." George may react in one of several ways. An appropriate response would be for him to paraphrase back to her what she said with something like, "I hear that you would like to spend more quality time together."

More likely, however, he is going to do one of several things. He might focus on the word never. "Never? *Never?* Are you trying to say I never take you out? Six weeks ago, I took you to McDonald's, and now I've 'never' taken you out. Is that what you are trying to say?"

Another tactic that he may use is to fight back using correct principles. He may say something like "What? Don't you believe we need to be frugal? We've had enough fights over the budget. Don't you believe our budget is important?"

His wife cannot argue with that principle, of course, but she may retort with another principle. "But don't you believe in the quality of our relationship and that we should spend quality time together?" Of course, how can anyone argue with either one of these principles? However, it's the purpose behind them that is the problem; they are being used to beat up one another. We can be right in principle and wrong in practice.

• **Don't say, "I told you so" or anything similar.** The natural man is certainly an enemy to God and to everyone else around. Many of us face situations in which we'd love to utter the words, "I told you so!" It never helps!

• **If one person has a communication problem, you both have a communication problem.** In family therapy, it can be difficult for people to take responsibility for their own behaviors. We get busy tending one another's doorsteps and miss our own.

• **It is against the rules to tell another person when they are breaking the rules.** You can't have somebody on the team with a whistle. This is annoying. People are not going to be perfect, but I do not want the rules or guidelines to become another problem.

I have always enjoyed a beautiful recitation called "All I Ever Needed to Know, I Learned in Kindergarten." Here it is in its entirety:

ALL I REALLY NEEDED TO KNOW,
I LEARNED IN KINDERGARTEN

Most of what I really need to know about how to live, and what to do, and how to be, I learned in kindergarten. Wisdom was not at the top of the graduate school mountain, but there in the sand box at nursery school. These are the things I learned. Share everything. Play fair. Don't hit people. Put things back where you found them. Clean up your own mess. Don't take things that aren't yours. Say you are sorry when you hurt somebody. Wash your hands before you eat. Flush. Warm cookies and cold milk are good for you. Live a balanced life. Learn some and think some and draw some and paint and sing and dance and play and work every day.

Take a nap every afternoon. When you go out in the world, watch for traffic, hold hands, and stick together. Be aware of wonder. Remember the little seed in the plastic cup? The roots go down and the plant goes up and nobody really knows how or why. We are like that. And then remember that book about Dick and Jane and the first word you learned, the biggest word of all: LOOK! Everything you need to know is there somewhere. The Golden Rule and love and basic sanitation, ecology, and politics and the sane living.

Think of what a better world it would be if we all, the whole world, had cookies and milk about three o'clock every afternoon and then lay down with our blankets for a nap. Or we had a basic policy in our nation and other nations to always put things back where we found them and clean up our own messes. And it is still true, no matter how old you are, when you go out in the world, it is best to hold hands and stick together.[49]

Chapter Nine:

BE CYNICAL, BLAME OTHERS, AND TRUST NO ONE

MY OFFICE IS DECORATED WITH clowns. They partly represent the masks that we all wear, but they also remind us of the need for a sense of humor. People who are depressed often lose their sense of humor. Nothing seems funny to them. When they first come into my office, they often feel they are being judged, so they take pains to put on their masks in exactly the right way.

I often encourage these people to laugh at their situations. Recently, a man from a small Idaho community came in bemoaning his problems with isolation and alienation. "I have just talked with another fellow from your same town," I said. "He too felt quite depressed. He had even gotten himself to a point of suicide but had decided against it because, living where he did, suicide would only be redundant." He was able to laugh, and this helped break the ice.

Humor opens people up to talk about their feelings and, more importantly, helps them talk about their fears and apprehensions in an indirect way. In fact, I think humor is critical to my success as a therapist. Starting to see a therapist and taking off your emotional clothes, so to speak,

125

and letting your vulnerable side be seen may be threatening. If we can add humor and lighten things up by letting ourselves be seen as more human, we've won part of the battle.

I tell some patients that anybody who would see me ought to have their head examined! I want them to feel that we can have an open relationship. In the end, some of the therapeutic process has some friendship and parenting to it.

Of course, there's much more to humor than breaking the ice. Again, many depressed people have lost their ability to have fun, and this does not go unnoticed by the people around them. When laughter, humor, and smiling have left peoples lives, they become cynical, guarded, and distrustful. Life has become joyless and previous interests are discontinued. Somehow, depressed people become so wrapped up in their own emergencies, crises, and burdensome lives that they no longer identify with others. They most often become self-centered, justifying their thoughts and feelings because of the tragedies in their lives. Typically, they feel that no one cares for them. Many times, they have stopped serving and caring for others. They have shut themselves up in their homes, stopped attending gatherings of their peers and friends, and spend their time alone.

Some years ago I heard the following from the pulpit:

> *When you're not hanging on your own cross, you should be praying at the feet of someone else's.*[50]

That statement tells us a great deal about suffering and charity and the way our Heavenly Father and Savior feel about them. It in no way implies that our personal suffering is not painful or consuming; however, it recognizes the cyclic process of good and bad, happy and sad, that we each go through and reminds us not to forget that others suffer too.

People sometimes speak of putting up walls. This is a way of expressing that they don't trust anyone or that they don't let people know the real them. We've all been hurt by others, and I can understand why people feel the need for these walls. I'm certainly not suggesting that we don't have a right to our pain, but I am suggesting it doesn't benefit us or anyone else to pin that pain to our sleeves like a war badge, refusing to let it go.

You may be familiar with a helpful acronym—FIDO—which stands for Forget It and Drive On! We might all benefit from this counsel.

I have counseled several patients who have been victims of sexual abuse. When these people realize what has happened to them, they experience a myriad of emotions including anger, betrayal, and confusion. Often they want the perpetrator to be punished. However, many times these victims do not come forward; some don't even realize they were victimized until later in adulthood. By that time, the abuser has often died or is quite elderly.

I counseled one particular patient who was in such a difficult situation. She had started having flashbacks at about age twenty-eight and had no idea what they meant. Through therapy and talking to other siblings, she discovered that her flashbacks were real—she had been sexually abused by her father. Sexual abuse is tragic under any condition, but her situation was rather unique. Her father was an elderly man, and she had the responsibility of taking care of him during his final years.

She experienced the anger, denial, and desire that her father pay for what he had done, or at least be confronted with his deeds. However, her father was many years into a battle with Parkinson's disease with its accompanying dementia.

"If you confronted your father, would he remember what he has done?" I asked her one day.

She answered, "No."

"Then," I told her, "you have a choice. You can remain angry and feel victimized, or you can turn it over to the Lord and FIDO."

She pondered this for nearly three weeks before she had the courage to turn judgment over to the Lord. She forgot it and moved on. She spent the last eight years of her father's life giving him quality care and tender loving attention. A triumph to be sure!

There are two general ways to forget. One way is through a brain injury. The other is to stop paying attention to, brooding over, and exerting energy toward the memory you want to forget.[51]

Rachel lit a cigarette as she sat in her apartment all alone. "I'm never going to overcome this," she cried in despair. "I just keep trying and failing. I give up!" A convert of two years, Rachel had little by little returned to smoking during the past year. She tried to stop several times, only to start again every time. "Smoking is my relief from stress" she told me. In her shame and discouragement, she stopped going to church. "I know people can smell it on me," she told herself, remembering how one couple had glanced at each other in disapproval after she sat down by them the previous Sunday. "I'm not worthy to attend church anymore," she told herself dejectedly.

We have all been hurt. Someone says something or does something, either on purpose or by accident, which brings us up short. We're surprised, shocked, angry, hurt, offended, violated, or embarrassed. What are you going to choose to do? You have a choice.

Each of us has heard the opposing voices within our own heads, that critical voice that Rachel heard telling her she wasn't worthy. What is the source of thoughts and feelings like these? Is this the encouraging voice of the Savior that calls to us?

> *Come unto me, all ye that labour and are heavy laden, and*
> *I will give you rest.* (Matthew 11:28)

Or is this the voice and influence of that being that seeks to discourage us and destroy all that is good?

Many of us have heard the term GIGO; it stands for Garbage In, Garbage Out. If we think of our brain as the largest, most sophisticated computer imaginable, we can better understand the relationship between what we enter into our computer and what comes out of it. If we fill our brain with negative, defeating, or sarcastic information, we have to realize that these same types of information are going to come out in our speech, our thoughts, and our actions.

One of my specialties as a psychologist is that of a suicidologist. I often work with coroners on unusual cases. I have come to realize that impaired reality testing is the cause of most of these tragic suicides. Why? If your reality testing tells you that not being able to pay your property taxes means you and your family will lose your home, you might find yourself despairing and devastated. Unfortunately, you may associate this thought with "I can't stand that. There is no solution . . . I just want to die!"

If you, as a child, believe that your parents love their possessions more than they love you, you might become devastated by a fender-bender accident or a mishap in the home where something gets broken. These feelings and thoughts of guilt and shame can become so overwhelming that you might think, "My dad will kill me! He'll disown me! I can't stand the possible outcome . . . I just want to die."

Some time ago, I was called to the home of an eleven-year-old boy who had apparently taken his own life with a high-powered rifle. There were no indications of a note, and the boy had seemed a happy member of an integrated family. What had caused this seemingly intelligent and well-adjusted youngster to turn the rifle on himself? It turned out that he had stayed home from school and had apparently become bored and began playing with his dad's shotgun and rifle. The shotgun accidentally discharged, blowing a hole in a piece of antique furniture. I suspect that in the ensuing moments, the fear of the wrath and embarrassment he anticipated terrified him to the extent that he killed himself. I don't know why his reality testing failed him that day, but I know that many, many people find themselves suicidal because of cognitive distortions.

Many of our Heavenly Father's children who face crises do not have the benefit of the gospel in their lives to help them bridge these experiences. The reality for them may be that they don't have a sense of their own intrinsic worth. They have only the insight to see themselves as they believe others see them to be. What a tragedy! Most religions have three basic psychological purposes

1. To help us face hardships, death, upset, losses, and sicknesses. Religion gives us faith and coping skills for dealing with tragedies.
2. To provide fellowship with other people who are supportive and kind and who provide a support system when we need it.
3. To provide the promotion and framework for civility.

In the Book of Mormon, the prophet Alma set up the Lord's church in the land of Mormon. He tells us what we are required to do for ourselves and others if we wish to be part of God's Church and what we can expect in return:

> *And now, as ye are desirous to come into the fold of God, and to be called his people, and are willing to bear one another's burdens, that they may be light; Yea, and are willing to mourn with those that mourn; yea, and comfort those that stand in need of comfort, and to stand as witnesses of God at all times and in all things, and in all places that ye may be in, even until death, that ye may be redeemed of God, and be numbered with those of the first resurrection, that ye may have eternal life. . . . And they were called the church of God, or the church of Christ from that time forward. . . . And he commanded them that they should observe the sabbath day, and keep it holy, and also every day they should give thanks to the Lord their God. (Mosiah 18:8–9, 17, 23)*

Any organization (and the Church is an organization) consists of four distinct components:

1. Doctrines, creeds, and basic beliefs
2. Traditions and practices
3. The people—members
4. Personal preferences and individual opinions

In any religion it is helpful to keep these four things separate. This is one of the reasons that Latter-day Saint Church leaders constantly recommend scripture study. If we are well-grounded in scriptural doctrines, we can weed out of our lives the overwhelming array of personal beliefs or ideas that members may present as doctrine.

For instance, there is a huge difference between the law of chastity and the "law" some people propose of not kissing at all before marriage. We can rightfully be exact about keeping God's laws, but we also need to see the significant difference between His laws and other people's opinions.

While the Articles of Faith set the tenets of our religion on paper in a simple and understandable way, actually comprehending the core doctrines of the Latter-day Saint religion and its complexities requires a lifetime of study and prayer.

Certainly, we understand and can accept at face value that our society includes smart people, dumb people, rigid people, flexible people, and everything in between. Sometimes we take what we observe at face value and try to interpret it as right or wrong, good or bad, righteous or unrighteous. However, people get hung up on this principle or that principle, this doctrine or that doctrine, and try to preach on the basis of a single or a select few principles, ignoring the tremendous mass of other equally important doctrines.

A few examples of personal behavior or tradition that may cause confusion include the following:

• You are at a civic event and the flag is presented. Your tradition is that you should put your hand over your heart when the flag is presented. However, some of those around you not only don't put their hand over their heart, but they don't even take their hats off or stop talking! You attach a label to these people as unpatriotic or as bad Americans.

• You attend a funeral for an acquaintance in your neighborhood. There is no special musical number, no doctrinal discussion of life after death. The meeting is just short and sweet. Later, you tell other people how weird the funeral was and indicate that it just didn't feel right or reverent.

• You have been in the same area for many years and have come to expect that your bishoprics shouldn't have facial hair, that they sit in the same place on the stand each week, and that the leaders of the Church always wear dark suits. You get a new bishopric, and the counselors both have facial hair. What's more, they decide a few weeks after being called that they want to sit on the right side instead of the left side behind the podium. To your greater shock, one of the counselors has a light green suit and he sometimes wears it with penny loafers! Without meaning to, you start withdrawing your support of that ecclesiastical leadership because of the way they dress, look, and where they sit on the stand.

• You attend Sacrament meeting one Sunday and note that the cloth on the sacrament table is off-white and that the sacramental bread is whole-wheat instead of white. You refuse to partake of the Sacrament because of the "blasphemy."

• You have some good friends in the area who just made a huge change in their family organization. Now they have the dad staying home with the children and the mom going out as the breadwinner. Soon you start to see problems with some of their children, and you determine that they are breaking the Lord's commandment by having the mother work and the father stay home. After all, "no other success can compensate for failure in the home," right?[52]

• You move into a new area. You recall that in the area you came from, all the young men became Eagle scouts and received their Duty to God award. However, in this new area, scouting doesn't seem to play an important role in the young men's program and not many of the young men become Eagle scouts. You determine that this ward is not as in tune and as righteous as the ward you came from and determine that the young men and their leaders are just not living right.

• You like to take notes during Sacrament meeting so you can have them to refer back to. However, after several weeks of doing this, you review your notes and find that you feel worthless or substandard as a result of the talks and how you compare yourself to everyone else. One Sunday, the talks were on family home evening, another week on temple attendance, another week on family scripture study, and still another on keeping the Sabbath Day holy. Yet, none of the people who spoke did things the way your family does them, and so you are certain that you have fallen out of grace with God. After all, if you aren't having weekly family home evening, daily family scripture reading, attending the temple every week, and if you happen to watch television on Sunday, you truly must be a heathen, right?

In a meeting I attended several years ago, a member addressed the subject of repetition in prayer. The good man stated that a person should never utter more than two references to the Lord or Heavenly Father during a prayer because that is repetitious (using the second commandment in Exodus 20 as a reference). However, later that same week during a general media broadcast from Salt Lake, the General Authority giving the opening prayer gave a tender but pleading invocation. He used the phrase Father in Heaven numerous times in somewhat of a pleading way. After the prayer, I asked a friend, "Do you think God was truly offended by that invocation because his name was stated so many times?"

I sometimes refer to this as people having their hobbies in the Church. Another example of someone practicing their hobbies in a stake position (that is their personal preferences, biases, prejudices, and bigotries) is a stake president I knew at one time who stated that he wanted no men in his stake to have any facial hair. He stated that he didn't think that this was the way LDS men should present themselves. Now, when we look at the whole picture, I feel he was missing several things. First of all, this was HIS hobby. As the stake president, I guess he did have the right to this point of view, but as members, do we not have the right to our own personal inspiration? I know a man, for example, who has a badly deformed upper lip from surgery when he was a youth. He wears a mustache, nicely trimmed. Should we deprive him of that camouflage? Further, I know a man who had severe acne as a youth and has pockmarks. He has a well-trimmed beard, and it looks nice. Should we deprive him of that camouflage?

Many of us have these little biases and prejudices. However, we should keep in mind the counsel we have already referred to from Doctrine and Covenants 121:

> *No power of influence can or ought to be maintained*
> *by virtue of the priesthood, only by persuasion, by long-*
> *suffering, by gentleness and meekness, and by love*
> *unfeigned.* (D&C 121:40)

Valerie came into my office feeling very worried. Like many Latter-day Saints, she had a strong commitment to living the gospel. Unfortunately, she wasn't well grounded in Church doctrine. Therefore, she relied heavily on what she was told by members of the Church. She was distressed because a member had told her that since her father had been cremated instead of buried in the traditional Mormon way, it was very possible that his salvation was in jeopardy as well as the family unit in the hereafter. The family member who had helped make this "wrong decision" had jeopardized the whole family. "The body is a temple," the member had said, "and cremation certainly doesn't respect that truth."

To compound Valerie's problem, another member felt compelled to add that it was also disrespectful to pierce your ears. She said that if the Lord wanted us to wear earrings we would be born with holes in our ears and that to desecrate or mutilate the body in any way would certainly be against God's will. Because Valerie believed these women, she had been suffering unnecessary guilt and anxiety. She was more than relieved when I assured her that these members' opinions on those issues were *not* Church doctrine.

While many of these traditions or personal views may be the norm within our society, variances from them certainly doesn't make you or me less valuable to our Heavenly Father. He loves us *all* the time, not just some of the time. I would hope that each of us would be very careful about so condemning or judging another person. To cause another person even one minute's panic and anxiety over personal beliefs and traditions certainly can't be what Heavenly Father wants of his children.

When I first became a bishop, I was called to the office of a very kind and loving stake president. We talked at length about the office of a bishop with its responsibilities, duties, trials, and joys. At the end of my interview, the stake president asked if I had any questions. I replied that I had enough questions to keep us both at his office for many years. He kindly asked me to give him some examples. I told him about a couple who had bought a house for $35,000. It was an inflationary time in our history and, over the next six years, the house inflated to a point that it was worth nearly $60,000. They had made some improvements in the home, but when they sold it, they had recognized $20,000 of inflationary gains. They moved to another town where housing costs were more than double and bought a house for $90,000; this house was only two-thirds the size of the one that they sold. I said to him, "Now, President, we are supposed to pay tithing on our increase. They did increase but then they decreased. Should they have paid tithing on this $20,000 of inflated money from the sale of the first home?" This gentle stake president responded politely, "I don't know."

I then told of a woman who had some serious physical problems and had been encouraged by several doctors not to have any more children. However, there was one doctor who told her it might be hard but may be achieved with medical supervision and discipline. She desperately wanted more children. I asked quietly, "President, should I have instructed her to have more children?" Again he replied, "I don't know."

After asking several of these questions, I was somewhat frustrated; after all, the Stake President had asked if I had any questions. Gathering courage, I finally said, "President, in this area of the Lord's vineyard, you are my answer man. If you don't have the answers to these questions, who does?"

The stake president smiled and said gently, "Oh, that's easy. You can go into any Relief Society or any quorum and somebody there will give you an answer."[53]

My gentle, loving, and kind stake president wasn't suggesting that we should poll the ward or the world for answers to our individual questions; he was saying that there is no manual of absolutes. We have to interpret quietly with our spouses and within ourselves what is right.

The Lord has provided guidelines. We have been given our agency, good minds, access to inspiration, and the ability to pray. To turn ourselves over to other people to make these kinds of decisions is simply not God's will. Rigidly living according to the letter of the law preempts our ability to live the higher laws of love.

I have been in numerous LDS church courts. Most were conducted with love and concern. Despite that, I have known members who have fallen away because of misunderstandings and hurt feelings.

The Church provides the continuity and stability we require in this confusing and unstable world. I have yet to see someone benefit from falling into inactivity and withdrawing from God's kingdom.

Perhaps a good caption for this next cartoon would be: "When you find you are digging yourself into a hole, STOP DIGGING!"

We all wear masks to some degree from time to time and in some situations. We have all been told to "put on a happy face." This is probably the most appropriate mask. So many depressed people come in and report that people don't like them, don't want to be around them, or are avoiding them. That is a rather predictable consequence when you look at their sad, flat, unemotional demeanor. Other masks may be just as alienating and just as phony—masks such as I don't care about you, I'm tough, I'm indifferent, and I don't need anybody. These masks are equally destructive.

We all have to recognize that we have hidden feelings and hurts, and we need to learn to deal with them if we are going to resolve them. Sometimes with the right people and in the appropriate places, it is all right to take off our emotional clothes. It may feel awkward and uncomfortable, but it is critical for proper evaluation and therapy. It should, however, be done with discrimination and discernment.

SEEING INSIDE THE CLOWN

Can you see outside your window
At the people passing by?
And did you ever wonder
If they laugh, or cry, or sigh?
Do they carry little smiles
Turned up upon their face?
Did you wonder if those smiles
Life's pain does now replace?
Let's look more deeply at the eyes.
Let's look with hearts that care.
Perhaps we'll find what's hiding—
What turmoil might be there.
Can we take away the masks now?
And even facial paint?
Can we tell them we still love them?
They don't have to play the Saint?
Maybe these are the subtle
Painted clowns that we all love,
And maybe they'll remove their masks
If we handle with "kid" gloves![54]

At times we all go through discouragement, alienation, self-derogation, and depression. At times we may feel others are judging us. During these times, we must have someone we can trust. However, because of our pain, we don't want to let anyone in, and we build walls that are incredibly high. Many of us assume that we are good communicators and that we are safe to talk to. In reality, however, many of us are not.

Everyone is in need of a confidant, someone you can tell anything to. Your confidant may not be able to make things better, but he certainly shouldn't make things worse! How can we make a trusted communication worse and, thereby, proving ourselves a poor confidant? Read the "oops" list below and see if you break the rules of being a trusted confidant:

1. Telling others: If I confide in you, and you tell other people, you betray my confidence. Hence, you aren't a very good confidant.
2. Compounding the negative feelings: I tell you something that I feel bad, guilty, or stupid about. Then after telling you, I feel even worse. This does not make you a good confidant.
3. Dredging up the past: You handle what I share with you well initially, but days or weeks later, you bring it and slap me in the face with it! You are not a good confidant!

Perhaps we have learned from sad experience that good confidants are, indeed, hard to find.

Chapter Ten

DISH IT OUT
BUT DON'T
TAKE IT

DEPRESSED PEOPLE HAVE LOW TOLERANCES for ambiguity, things being out of place, and mild frustrations. People who have psychological tendencies toward perfection need structure and get rigid or hyper-regulated about trivial things (a clean garage, everything being in its place, unspotted cars, and the dishes being loaded in the dishwasher correctly, to name a few).

Overwhelmed parents sometimes get involved with trying to teach correct principles but in doing so totally alienate themselves from their children. Perfectionistic people often become critical, even angry when circumstances or the behaviors of others around them are chaotic, unstructured, or not going as they think they ought to be going. All of these might be reasons someone would become angry. There are five general ways that people handle anger:

1. The pressure-cooker type. They are often the life of the party and everybody's best friend. But they have a dark little secret. After being passive, passive, passive, they explode into fits of anger without warning.

They are sorry later, after they have left numerous injured souls reeling in their wake. Many times they say things like, "He made me mad." This is somehow supposed to defend or license the explosion and justify misbehavior.

For example, a young mother in her early thirties came in with her three-year-old son. While we were talking, the boy ran all over my office, touching things, bumping things together, and looking into things. I was very uneasy about this, but I felt that it was the mother's job to intervene. This went on for about forty minutes, when all of a sudden she jumped up, grabbed the boy, swatted him harshly a couple of times, threw him down on the couch, and told him to sit there and mind his own business. The little boy looked up at her and said, "You're just being mean, Mommy." In his eyes, that was true. He did not correlate the spanking or her getting mad at him with any of his behavior. He thought it happened randomly, without any thought; it was just explosive. All he saw was her anger; he never got the lesson.

People who explode are either defined as enemies or they are discounted, discredited, and devalued. That is, they are going to see the anger and explosiveness and determine that the one exploding is the one having the problem, totally missing the message, thinking rather, "She must be having a bad day," "She must be having PMS," or "He must not feel good today."

2.   The passive aggressive or passive resistant type. While this behavior differs dramatically from the pressure-cooker, the behavior is equally damaging. A passive aggressive type refuses to argue with anyone; he avoids conflict. The passive resistant type sometimes has what we refer to as Donkey Syndrome. If you are in a hurry, they go slower. They don't get mad; they get even. They are the ones who would literally sit in a building and burn it down around them, just to make a point. They cut off their nose to spite their face. They are so caught up in being right that they forget individual choice, accountability, and flexibility, and will often claim to have never been angry. The problem with this is that it keeps the skin chafed, so to speak. While there is no explosion, everyone feels the tension and is terribly on edge.

3.   The passive type. This person feels and acts like a doormat because he takes things, and takes things, and takes things, and never responds. The problem with this is that people internalize the anger and end up with physical problems such as headaches, ulcers, spastic colon, and even fibromyalgia.

4.   The aggressive or explosive type. If they don't like what is going on, these people will run over the top of others physically, verbally, or in any other aggressive fashion. The aggressive person often loses his job, gets a divorce, or ends up in jail or prison.

5.   The assertive type. This type correctly deals with anger. However, many people confuse assertiveness with aggressiveness, and often people who claim to be assertive are being mean and abrupt and consequently aggressive. Those who are assertive exemplify two major qualities: They use the correct guidelines for problem-solving (no yelling, no screaming, no name calling, etc.), and, most importantly, they are consistent.

We've covered the five ways that people handle anger. There are also common traps that most of us fall into day after day. As you read this list of some of the more common thinking errors, think about the communications and relationships you have. See if you can identify times when you have fallen into these traps. I believe knowledge is power, and the more you know, the more power you have over your own life:

- **Anger:** Using anger to control and manipulate others through emotional blackmail, aggression, attacking, and criticizing. An attempt to make others avoid confronting us with our behavior, allowing us to avoid responsibility for our behavior.
- **Assuming:** Believing that we know what others are thinking and feeling, then responding to that belief without checking it out.
- **Blaming:** Shifting responsibility to others for our actions. We might admit our actions were wrong, but we insist it was not our fault and that we should not be held responsible.
- **Drama:** Manipulating others into a fight for amusement or to divert attention away from our own behavior.
- **Helplessness:** Whining and making such statements like, "I am too stupid to do anything for myself." Other statements might include, "I can't (which really means I won't)," "I didn't know," "I didn't understand," "I don't get it."
- **Entitlement:** Believing that our problems are so unique and different from anyone else's that no one can understand or help us and the rules and treatment don't apply to us.
- **Intellectualization:** Using academic, abstract, or theoretical discussions to avoid dealing with feelings or the real issue.
- **Justification:** Insisting that a behavior was not wrong for us to do because of extenuating circumstances.
- **Lying:** Telling lies to confuse, distort, and take the focus off

our behavior. Can be used in three forms:

A. **Commission:** Making something up that is not true.

B. **Omission:** Saying nothing, or telling a partial truth but leaving out important details.

C. **Assent:** Allowing someone to believe something happened in a way it did not, or going along with someone else's lie.

- **Minimizing:** Making our behavior seem less important than it is or discounting the significance of the behavior.
- **Deflecting:** Shifting the focus to avoid dealing with the real issue.
- **Vagueness:** Purposely being unclear and nonspecific to avoid being pinned down and held responsible.
- **Victim playing:** Presenting as a victim to avoid being held responsible for your hurtful behaviors.

Statistical data are always interesting and fun, but one should not jump to conclusions. Observation is easy; interpretation is difficult. When giving suicide lectures, for instance, I point out that Des Moines, Iowa, and Boise, Idaho, both have a notorious reputation. Both cities have high suicide rates with the number of deaths by suicide much greater than the surrounding areas or the surrounding counties.

Okay . . . your brain is already trying to solve this riddle. Why would two nice cities like Des Moines, Iowa, and Boise, Idaho, have this kind of death record by suicide? Let me help. Both of these cities have trauma centers. Suicide victims are often life-flighted from miles away into both cities where they are pronounced dead immediately or within a few days, instead of being pronounced dead where they may have actually overdosed or injured themselves.

What did you think when you read the statistic about Boise and Des Moines? Some might conclude, "It must be smog, bigger populations, alienation, traffic, crime, and other stresses." Did you come up with conclusions with little or no information? Remember, observation is easy; interpretation is difficult!

There are other types of statistics and, of course, someone is always ready to jump on the bandwagon for or against something without enough information to bake a cake. Here are a few of them: A recent study came out that said that women who have taken antibiotics for more than five hundred days in the past twenty years have higher rates of breast cancer. Of course, the bandwagon immediately concluded that antibiotics cause cancer. Actually, those who take antibiotics may be more fragile and susceptible to disease in general. Thus, it may not be the antibiotic use but may be that these people have impaired immune systems.

A few years ago a medical study reported that people who drank a "moderate" amount of alcohol lived healthier and longer. They initially concluded that the alcohol extended life. Later they concluded it was not the alcohol; it was the "moderation." People who drink moderately also tend to eat and live moderately.

A cute conclusion in old Switzerland ought to bring a chuckle: The officials noted that the birth rate increased dramatically in the spring and summer when storks were nesting on the roofs in Switzerland. Thus, people formed the conclusion that storks bring babies. Although storks nest on the roofs in the early summer and that is when the birth rate normally goes up, the cause for the increase in birth rate is that in the fall, the crops are in and people have more time together, and, thus, more babies are conceived. I don't mean to alarm anyone, but storks do not cause or bring babies! We can see that it is important to not over-interpret, jump to conclusions, or make false assumptions about statistical information.

Statistics truly can get confusing. Many people believe that correlation implies causation, and it may. But it may just imply correlation. For example, the storks on the roofs in Switzerland like the rise and fall of the Boise River and hot dog sales in Yankee Stadium are correlated. When the river is at its highest, hot dog sales are also at their highest at Yankee Stadium, but they do not cause one another. They both come at the same time, mid-summer—the causation.

To help people confront their belief systems, I ask them to do an exercise where they list a series of beliefs they have held to this point in their lives. I have them break these beliefs down into categories like general philosophy, marriage, church, work, money, sex, men, women, children, parents, and self-concept.

Because God granted us agency and the power to choose, which takes us out of the victim role, we do not have to be emotionally attached to, bigoted by, or prejudged by our past beliefs. Through confronting and carefully examining our beliefs, we can choose new ways of thinking and believing. The following example gives a taste of the kinds of results I see when people complete this exercise:

OLD BELIEFS	NEW BELIEFS
WORK Anything worth doing is worth doing well. If you can't do it right, don't do it.	WORK Some things are worth doing well. Some are worth doing for fun. Some things aren't even worth doing.
SELF-CONCEPT You're just like _____ (define).	SELF-CONCEPT I have _____'s eyes and sense of humor, but I am different in other respects such as _____ (define your list).
GOD God loves me when I am good.	GOD God loves me and would like me to do right for my own happiness.
LIFE Good things never last.	LIFE Things change—the taste of something good doesn't last, but I can enjoy the moment.
SEX Sex is only for procreation.	SEX Sex is for many things such as communication, bonding, expressions of love, and procreation. Monogamous animals that mate for life have frequent sex and not just for procreation.

When we were young, perhaps we had no real choices and did not have enough information or life experiences to decide or to conclude anything about our actions. However, as adults, we can choose (listen to the power of that word) to believe how we are going to think, feel, and act. Isn't it a sad state when we realize that we have both the ability and the right to choose, but fail to extend those same rights and abilities to others?

Chapter Eleven

CONFUSE
ROMANCE
WITH LOVE

WHAT A FEELING! BUT CAN that first flash-dancing, knee-buckling sensation of falling in love endure? A number of papers and books have been written about falling in love. One description, written by Valerie Frankl, a columnist, concludes, "Turns out, I am mentally ill."[47] Some of the descriptions in our music seem particularly revealing: We walk on air, we fall head over heels, we're twitterpated, we're crazy.

Aspects in the brain chemistry of a person in love resemble that of a person with manic disorder.

A devastating thing that happens in life is when a young man and young woman meet and they really like one another. Science has shown us in these early stages of romance that we produce very stimulating hormones. This is why people in the early stages of a relationship can get by on little or no sleep. They often talk for endless hours about politics, religion, hopes, dreams, trips, and philosophies of various kinds.

However, later as marriage moves along and if it really settles down into a good relationship, couples actually produce more endorphins, and the relationship actually becomes more comfortable and sedate.

Conflict in marriage occurs when the nature of the discussed topics changes. Instead of talking about philosophies and dreams, they start to talk about the problems they have, (a hole in the roof, the squeaky washing machine, Johnny's bedwetting, Susie's grades, or the budget).

Depending on how things go, the couple might even visit a therapist and say such things as "I don't like to talk to him because it gives me a headache" or "When I come home and talk to her, it always gives me a stomachache."

Unless you're a masochist and enjoy pain and suffering, eventually you are going to start avoiding those kinds of topics. This becomes disastrous. We end up procrastinating and avoiding all talk.

A solution to this that seems to work is to schedule time every week and talk with a problem-solving agenda. We've talked about having these scheduled meetings in an earlier chapter. However, as repetition is the best teacher, I'd like to expand on that idea. Most people who have ever been in an elder's quorum presidency or a Relief Society presidency or a Bishopric, realize that in order to get things done, they must sit down every week and follow an agenda. This keeps them on track.

Some agenda items will, of course, carry over. New agenda items will be added and old ones deleted as problems are solved. During this critical meeting, assignments are made and timelines are outlined. For example, I will call George the handyman in our ward by Wednesday to have him come take a look at the hole in the roof. By Thursday I will have checked out prices on new blinds for the living room. You can see how a weekly meeting and problem-solving agenda can benefit you.

Much is said these days about love languages. Gary Chapman's landmark book, *The Five Love Languages*, is a valuable resource. However, I have added two additional languages of love to his original five. I've listed seven of love languages below:

1. Verbal—words of affirmation
2. Quality time
3. Gifts
4. Acts of service
5. Physical—touching and stroking
6. Loyalty and fidelity—not talking behind one another's backs
7. Respect—don't interrupt; use attending behaviors; honor opinions

It is not always necessary to take the scriptures literally or perform the letter of that law without paying full attention to what would really make the other person happy.

You may say, "What I'd like others to do unto me is to bring me chocolate chip cookies. So that's what I'm going to take to my neighbor." However, the neighbor may really like some other kind of cookie, such as gingersnaps or oatmeal and raisin. Maybe your neighbor is even allergic to chocolate! The key here is to recognize what other people want, not what we want.

The problem is, of course, our human nature. If a person isn't getting the service he wants, he may slack off and not give the words of affirmation or the warm, physical touch that his spouse is lacking.

Seek to understand before seeking to be understood!

Someone once told me:

I know you believe you understand what you think I said, but I am not sure you realize what you heard is not what I meant.

Others will relate this advice from the scriptures:

For if ye love them which love you, what reward have ye? do not even the publicans the same? (Matthew 5:46)

As relationships develop, we can simply judge them to see if they are healthy. So many times we enter into a relationship with someone that seems a perfect match. However, if the relationship develops into marriage, we find ourselves married to someone who is real-life flesh and blood and imperfect. Sometimes we complain vehemently about faults in other people. But when all the dust settles, it becomes fairly obvious that these faults have been one of our own greatest weaknesses all along.

There is a triangle to be considered when looking at any relationship:

WHAT DOES THE
RELATIONSHIP
DO FOR YOU?

WHAT DOES THE
RELATIONSHIP
NOT DO FOR YOU?

WHAT DO YOU *NEED* OR
WANT THE RELATIONSHIP
TO DO FOR YOU?

A husband and wife came to see me for marriage counseling. They often argued about principles and issues. One of his main complaints was her housekeeping. During one session, he told me, in front of his wife, how he had watched a pizza box lay on the kitchen table for five days. He would walk by the pizza box every day, keeping score. He used this as a primary example of her inadequacy in housekeeping. Then he shored up his arguments with principles such as "cleanliness is next to godliness" and "the Spirit of the Lord cannot be in an unkempt house." The issues in this example are small, but they created a major problem for this couple.

Let's look closer at the above example. How much time would it have taken this husband to drop the pizza box into the garbage? Instead, he tried to justify his bad feelings with evidence. If this husband had loving feelings for his wife, he would try to find ways to help her and support her in overcoming the bad housekeeping rather than looking for reasons to justify his bad feelings.

On the other hand, how hard would it be for the wife to simply put the box in the garbage? Under appropriate circumstances and in a caring environment, his principle of "don't you think we should put garbage away?" and her principle of "don't you think everyone should help?" are replaced with sensitivity, caring, and consideration—higher and more rewarding principles.

The situation could be anything—dishes on the side of the bed, clothes on the floor, shoes in the front room. This couple did not have a corner on the market as far as keeping score and pettiness were concerned. Somehow, they had forgotten why they got married, why they loved each other in the beginning. They forgot that they had married for better or worse and for sickness and in health, and seemed to forget that helping each other succeed and feel satisfied in their relationship was a key goal. Consequently, as a good member of the Church, this husband used the scriptures and principles to condemn and convict his wife, thus justifying his complaints. This is a trap that many people find themselves in, a way of elevating themselves above their mates and making them look and feel better about themselves while they tear down someone else.

I once saw a couple in which the husband was in jail for hurting one of their children. When he got out, we talked about the different ways that we show love to each other, and about the seven love languages I described above.

Like many couples, this couple found themselves in a position where their languages were not the same. It is like the chocolate chip cookie scenario; there is nothing wrong with him liking chocolate chip cookies or her liking oatmeal and raisin cookies. However, if they don't realize the difference in their preferences, they will be trying to say "I love you" in the wrong language.

It was hard for this man to understand that his wife wanted his service, respect, and quality time. On the other hand, verbal and physical love were important to him. While she was doing the dishes, he would come in and start kissing her, hugging her, and telling her how much he loved her and how pretty she was. Instead of making her feel attractive and appealing, he simply irritated her.

They did work out these problems. She was quite wise! "Okay," she said, "I can do the verbal and the physical love." And she would. She would sit on the couch next to him while he watched TV. She played with the back of his neck. She also provided a lot of verbal love, words of affirmation. But it was in her control.

On the other hand, he did two amazing things that helped her feel loved and cared for. They didn't have much money, and the two acts of service he did took a lot of time and a lot of serious devotion. First, while her car was an older car, he kept it immaculate for her. Her car looked like it had just come off the showroom floor. It was shampooed, waxed, and polished. It looked amazing.

Second, although they lived in a very modest home in a modest neighborhood, people literally stopped in front of their house to admire it because their yard was incredibly well kept. He manicured the grass and pruned the shrubs. He always kept the windows clean. Everything was spotless on the outside of their home. These things meant a lot to her.

I remember another couple I saw. Sam was a very faithful member of the Church; he conscientiously fulfilled his calling as a Sunday School teacher every week. He enjoyed this calling because it afforded him the opportunity to study, ponder, and pray in order to be prepared to teach the older youth each Sunday. Another thing that was very important to him, as a convert to the Church, was having his temple recommend. He took it very seriously. He sincerely felt "that when Christ comes he will meet those who are faithful in the temple" (see D&C 133:2; 42:6).

Sam also worked very hard to earn a good living. He had worked the same job for almost seven years as a marketing representative for a national tire company. He enjoyed rubbing shoulders with quality people and was in a position of possible advancement within the next couple of weeks.

Sam's wife, Janet, was a constant critic. She felt that her needs were not being met. From a financial standpoint, she worried and fretted about the bills, even though there was always plenty of money. There was also a substantial amount going into a retirement system.

Janet had a habit of complaining about Sam to different relatives and even to their older children. She would badmouth Sam, censuring him for all the things he didn't get done, all the things he did wrong, and everything he should change about himself. This was something that he just quietly tolerated, figuring it was just the way she was.

While his wife was away visiting family for several weeks, Sam traded their car for a new one, which was something they had discussed several times. He felt that he had gotten the deal he wanted, so he obligated them to a reasonably hefty monthly payment but one that they could definitely afford.

When Janet returned home from her trip, she was livid. She protested angrily for many days and maligned him to their children, the neighbors, and just about anyone who would listen. Finally, in an ultimate coup, she went to Sam's employer, complaining bitterly about Sam. She told him that Sam had a bad habit of overspending their budget and had pulled tricks like this one several times. Her criticism was so vehement that after she left, Sam's boss called and made an appointment with Sam for 8:30 a.m. Monday morning. He anticipated being promoted all weekend and was five minutes early for his appointment on Monday morning. When he sat down with his boss Monday morning, fully expecting this to be a terrific day, he was smiling from ear to ear. His boss extended his hand and without so much as an "I'm sorry" told Sam that because of his repu-tation in the community and other reports he had received, even from Sam's own wife, the firm would be letting him go. He was told to clear out his desk and that he would be escorted off the campus by 9:30 a.m.

Sam's hurt and pain was astounding. He greatly resented that Janet had gone behind his back with her complaint. The sting of it all stayed bitterly with him. He would not relinquish that pain. He considered all of this to be a severe act of disloyalty on Janet's part.

I have not told you the outcome of this situation. It could have gone either way; it was their decision, their future, and their agency, but, in similar situations, I have seen it go either way.

From a religious point of view, I want to state that counseling, reprogramming, willingness to change, and the power of the Savior's love can turn these situations around. If both husband and wife want to stop the contention, are willing to repent, are willing to forgive, and will take the time and effort to "start over," "go back," "move forward," and "push past the pain and mistakes" of the past, their hearts can be changed and the marriage saved. But I did say *if.*

Perhaps the reader is in some desperate situation in which he feels that his marital situation is coming apart. It is not unusual for people who are hurtling along toward divorce to come to counselors, and certainly there are numerous suggestions that we make which may help. Some ideas that may help those who are most vulnerable may not be easy to swallow. You who feel that the marriage or relationship you want so much is completely out of your control many times become manipulative. You may begin acting in a way you hope will allow you to hold your partner in the marriage or relationship, often against their will.

I remember seeing a husband and wife who were new to me in a clinical setting. They were having numerous arguments about divorce, the children, and finances. One day he was storming out of the house, and she literally threw her arms around him and started begging, pleading, and crying as he dragged her down the hall. Let's look at this for just a moment. How do you think she felt? Does the phrase "two cents waiting for change" bring a picture to your mind? How much do we despise some people that we should perhaps have pity for? Do you think that we are willing to stay in a marriage simply out of pity?

In our dating years when all that chemistry was going on and we could stay up most of the night talking, we would never have dreamed of using such manipulative acts as begging, pleading, groveling, manipulative guilt, or anger. What do you think it would have done to your partner if you had used such techniques in convincing them to marry you?

A friend of mine came and showed me a new car that he had purchased and was telling me what a great deal he had gotten on the car. I, in rather a cocky way, said, "Well, I guess the salesman really did his job." He looked at me in a way that said I had implied he had been a fool or had been duped. Seeing his face, I said, "Man, I'm really glad you got a good buy." But actually the salesman's job is to make you think you got a great buy. It really doesn't matter sometimes whether you did or didn't.

This holds true in our spouses and in our relationship to our spouses. I believe that my spouse is the best deal in town. I would be the village idiot or the village idiot's protégé to dump her. It would be disastrous from an emotional, family, and financial standpoint. Now, has she duped me? Possibly, but I love every minute of it.

So, anyone who is reading this and is desperate for advice, please keep that in mind. Get away from the pleading, begging, groveling, manipulative guilt, and anger. You must become a salesperson and convince your drifting spouse that you are the best deal in town. The best deal in town does not imply guilt, pity, or anger. What would it accomplish the salesman to use such techniques on you?

Sometimes we confuse need with love. Our music even implies this: "You are my sunshine, my only sunshine." "You light up my life" implies that I can't get it lit up without you. The word *need* is *dependency*. I realized early in my marriage that my wife doesn't need me. If I should die, she would pick up the banner and march on. Would I want it any different than that? I think not.

AFTER A WHILE

> After a while you learn the subtle
> difference between holding a hand
> and chaining a soul.
> And you learn that love doesn't
> mean leaning and company
> isn't security.
> (Kisses aren't contracts and presents
> aren't promises.)
> After a while you begin to accept your
> defeats with your head up and your
> eyes open, with the grace of a woman,
> not the grief of a child.
> And you learn to build your roads on today
> because tomorrow's ground is too uncertain
> and the inevitable has a way of crumbling in mid-flight.
> After a while you learn that even
> sunshine burns if you stand too long in one place.
> So, you plant your own garden and
> decorate your own soul, instead of
> waiting for someone else to bring you flowers.
> And you learn that you really can endure,
> that you really do have worth.
> You learn that with every good-bye comes the dawn."[56]

Chapter Twelve

FOCUS ON THE NEGATIVE: ACT LIKE A WHIPPED DOG

EVERY ONCE IN A WHILE we run into someone at church or in the grocery store who believes that when we ask how they are, we want them to tell us the truth. No! Reality is that we want a polite nod and a smile. In essence:

We don't want to hear about the labor pains; we just want to see the baby!

Well, not really, but you know the type—the-glass-is-half-empty kind of people. At times we have all gotten an earful from a person whom we casually ask how they are doing. Far too many of us can recite every bad thing that has happened to us in the last week, but we can't even remember five good things that have happened. We are a society in which the evening and morning news are full of the tragic, the sorrowful, the wars, the disasters, the poor, the homeless, and the disease-laden.

The newspapers put the worst of the worst on the front page as if it is the only noteworthy thing! Back on page 16E or further, if we take the time to read that far, we might find a letter to the editor or an Ann Lander's article that touches our hearts and talks about something gentle or uplifting.

Is it any wonder that so many of us have something negative to say? Is it any wonder sometimes that our youth are sarcastic, facetious, frivolous, game-playing, television-watching, depressed people who can't see anything to look forward to and often feel hopeless?

How many of us would like to turn back the clocks and have our kids grow up in the simplicity of the sixties, when all we had to worry about was psychedelic drugs, love children, and cultists who convinced their congregations to commit mass suicide? The sixties were no easier to live in than the eighties or the early twenty-first century. The sixties had the Vietnam War, the eighties had gas lines and oil embargoes, and the twenty-first century has its share of trouble and concern. But, let me say this for the record: The youth of today are the brightest, strongest, smartest, and best prepared generation ever to grace this wonderful earth! They need us to be positive, hopeful, happy, enterprising, loving, patient, kind, and optimistic! This is a wonderful world we live in!

The way I see it, knowing ourselves is our first job. When we know who we are and what we want, we may find that our other relationships fall into place. It is best to be familiar with our core self and be actively engaged in nurturing it in directions we want to go in our lives. When we uncover this core and accept it and work on it, a more calm, stable, and secure self emerges, full of confidence and self-acceptance. Life then has purpose and happiness, while depression and hopelessness are less evident.

Every once in a while we meet people who tend to be critical. I had a close relative who often devastated those vulnerable to him. No matter what decision you made, he would find something wrong with it. If he found out you had bought a new car, he was quick to tell you what a stupid decision that was, reminding you of the excessive depreciation that would occur in just a few miles. However, if you bought a car that was just a couple of years old with low mileage, he would likewise find fault with it. "Why would someone sell a practically new car? It must have been a lemon. Somebody just sold you their problems. What a fool!"

Of course, if you bought an old car, he would point out that old cars simply fall apart. "Now you're going to be throwing more good money away. Old cars are undependable and a safety worry to boot. How could someone possibly put their family in danger like that?"

As you can see, my uncle always had a way of making you feel a bit off. Most people who knew him learned to overlook him while discounting his opinions. While they may have listened to him in a tolerant way, most people didn't incorporate his ideas. His friends were respectful toward him without taking his judgments to heart. But what about those few who, because of fragile egos or lack of confidence in their own decisions, listened to him and allowed themselves to become depressed, angry, and hurt? These are very vulnerable to faultfinding people like my uncle.

We all want other people to like and approve of us. As long as this is only a want, this may be acceptable. But when we decide that this approval is a dire necessity or an absolute need, we have set ourselves up for a lot of pain and suffering.

We often hear people ask someone, "Don't you have any self-respect?" But more often than not, they're talking about "other-respect." There is no more valuable exercise than to think through how much of your core self-respect is built upon how others see you. If your self-respect model is something superimposed from parents or peers, or if it double binds or negates you, it may well be alien to your true self. Let's bring our discussion around to the assertion that

Men are that they might have joy. (2 Nephi 2:25)

Bitterness, deprivation, overworking, and guilt are not joy. Trying to deal with someone who never lets you be happy and who is always finding fault with what you do is difficult and challenging.

Having said this, I'm not sure what a self-respect or self-esteem model is. I can tell you what it isn't—it is not all analytical. We can't define it with only words, because part of it is pure feeling, a quiet feeling of acceptance, independence, and understanding of our values. This, in turn, requires a good understanding of our strengths and weaknesses. Not surprisingly, a person with a well-integrated value system usually has measurable goals and consistent, identifiable values.

A self-esteem or self-respect model would also include having a good understanding and well-developed resources in reference to practical, physical, psychological, spiritual, and interpersonal things.

Let's turn to my relatives for another example, this time more positive. I have a cousin who will not listen to vulgar stories or ethnic jokes. He won't listen to any story or joke at the expense of any group. If someone starts to tell one, he walks away. If asked why he's leaving, he'll say he doesn't listen to stories like that. He doesn't chastise, he just leaves. I've noticed that his consistency in this has brought him "other-respect" even from those who do not share his sensitivities.

A model of self-respect is more than the sum of its parts. It really comes down to good feelings regarding a set of criteria, values, and beliefs. Its key component is a feeling that "I am going in the right direction. I am becoming okay, and the feeling that this is okay is coming from within and not from others."

I see many patients who are alienated from themselves. The difference between what a person would like to be and what we perceive ourselves to be is a fairly reliable indicator of our level of dissatisfaction with ourselves, or our level of depression. While not many people ever meet their ego ideal or what they would like to be, we cannot cope if we are too far removed from it.

Of course, some people's ego ideals are too rigid. Such people need to take an honest look at their efforts and abilities and realize that continuing to strive for the unreachable can have dangerous consequences.

Many people experience wide swings in self-esteem levels, depending on their context. A brain surgeon may feel good about himself only when he's doing brain surgery. Other people are on top of the world during the annual charity drive and feel lousy the other fifty-one weeks of the year. A healthy model of respect helps us feel good about ourselves even when we've made mistakes.

When I see a patient with a severe critical parent ego-state, armed with expressions like "idleness is the devil's workshop" and "time is money," I see how this keeps the eager to please adaptive-child ego-state constantly on the run. The workaholic, churchaholic, and motheraholic types are often literally being bombarded with threatening messages from the critical parent. Little wonder, then, that such people have difficulty when the kids leave home or other disrupting life events occur. Their respect and value is based on goals that become the sole basis of their existence.

When we focus on the negative and act like a whipped dog, we are inevitably brought to our knees. We need to realize the great power that we have inside ourselves, which is the ability to choose. When God gave us agency, he endowed us with enormous powers.

A few years ago, I went over to Eastern Idaho on a business trip. While I was there, I went to the cemetery where my parents and brother are buried. I lost my parents in my early youth and my brother when I was 25. I sat down on the graves for a while and began to bemoan the fact that my children had never met these people and that these people had never met or experienced my children or grandchildren. I thought of all the things that I had lost and they had lost. After doing this for about a half-hour, I had indeed whipped a good one on myself. Now we come to a reality here that most people must learn: If I have the ability to make myself worse—that is, more pitiful, angrier, more forlorn, sad, depressed, alienated, hurt—then I have the ability to make myself better.

Put on a happy face. That sounds simple, but there is some truth in that. Focusing on what is right is critical. It doesn't matter whether you focus on yourself, your spouse, or your children. Counting your many blessings works!

Chapter Thirteen

DENY THAT
RUST HAPPENS

SOMETIMES PEOPLE MISTAKENLY THINK THAT experience must be gained firsthand:

> *The only source of knowledge is experience.*[57]

Many of us have heard variations of this quote. I challenge the belief that we have to gain our knowledge from personal experience. How much better we are, if we are insightful and wise and are able to take the examples and experiences of others and learn from them.

I know a mother who explained the following about her small son: If he stubs his toe on the curb of the sidewalk outside of our house, he will look carefully at the place where he fell and will not stub his toe on that curb again. However, a block away, even within the same hour, he may stub his toe on another curb in much the same way. This child has learned through behavior modification that the curb outside his house requires him to pick up his feet carefully when walking. The child has yet to learn insight and wisdom regarding this principle. He may stub his toe many more times and in many more locations where the "curb" is slightly different.

What is it that distinguishes our learning and allows us to not simply react as Pavlov's dog[58] with behavior modification? How do we gain insight and wisdom that teach us to avoid all curbs on which we've actually stubbed our toes?

I am reminded of a story I heard when I was a boy:

INDIAN BOY AND THE SNAKE

A group of Arapaho Indian boys decided it was time to prove to the tribe elders that they were old enough to be considered men. By custom, the rite of manhood included living alone for one week in the wilderness. Each boy was instructed to only take a knife with him and come back seven days later and tell of his adventures. One boy, wanting to prove that he was more of a man than the others, decided that he would climb the snow-capped mountains for his week of adventure. Surely, living in the snow and cold is a hardship that the elders must agree that only a man could endure. So he walked an entire day across the plains to the foot of the mountains. He had climbed halfway up the mountains to the snowline when a snake spoke to him.

"Help me," the snake cried.

"Why should I help you, a rattlesnake? You are known to bite and kill people," replied the Arapaho brave.

"I am cold and almost frozen. Please put me in your warm shirt and take me down the mountain to where it is warm where I can survive," said the rattlesnake.

"How do I know that you are not going to bite and kill me?" asked the brave.

"Why should I bite the person who saves my life?" replied the snake.

"Okay. I do not like to see anyone die. Promise you won't bite me?" asked the brave.

"I promise," replied the snake.

So the Indian boy placed the snake in his shirt and walked down the mountain. As he opened his shirt to let the snake out, the rattlesnake bit him.

"WHY DID YOU BITE ME? You promised you wouldn't bite and kill me!" yelled the young brave.

The snake replied, "You knew who I was when you picked me up. You have nobody to blame for your death but yourself."[59]

Where did the young brave's reality testing fail him? Why did he risk helping a rattlesnake? What are some of the rattlesnakes in our own lives?

The name of this chapter is "Deny that Rust Happens." Let me give this example of why acquired knowledge does not stay fresh and motivating forever. Have you ever eaten a big meal for Thanksgiving or Christmas, maybe for your birthday at an all-you-can-eat Chinese buffet? You put into your body all types of delicious food. You finally stop eating when you are full; you probably couldn't eat another bite!

However, as full as you are at that moment, tomorrow you will be hungry again. Believe it or not, that wonderful, delightful, delicious, meal will not stay with you more than about twelve hours. You will eat again.

Knowledge is the same way. Although in November you read a book that filled your emotional and mental stomach, in March you will probably remember the feeling you had when you read that book but many, if not most, of the details will be lost to you. You may remember the subject matter, but unless you have taken specific steps to keep that knowledge fresh and motivating, you will eventually lose it.

There are several rather obvious ways that you can keep the information you acquire fresh and motivating.

- Take written notes while you read or listen to speakers.
- Write down quotes, sayings, and scriptures as you hear them.
- As you write down the quotes, say them out loud.
- Repeat scriptures and quotes out loud several times a week in order to commit them to memory.
- Make posters or charts with the thoughts that are most meaningful to you and place them around your home.
- While taking notes, be certain to list the source of the quote or scriptural reference.
- Relate an event or experience with information you are trying to remember, thus providing a jog to your memory, if and when needed.
- Put music to the information you are trying to learn. For instance, Janeen Brady is an author/composer and the founder of Brite Music. She was one of the first I was aware of that took information as simple as your phone number or address, applied music and repetition to it, and was successful at teaching even two-year-old children their phone numbers, including

area code. Many people have also learned all the books in the Old and New Testament by learning them with a catchy tune attached.

- Find pictures or graphics that go with the thing you are trying to remember. A picture that forever reminds me of the famous poem "Footsteps" is a beautiful picture of a beach alongside a sharp cliff. The sun is low in the brilliant sky, and in the ensuing evening you can see one set of footsteps in the sandy beach.

Another picture that prompts my memory of a famous quote is the picture of Christ standing at a door with no handle. The scripture says:

> *Behold, I stand at the door, and knock: if any man hear my voice, and open the door, I will come in to him, and will sup with him, and he with me.* (Revelation 3:20)

Experience, behavior modification, the example of others, repetition, and memory joggers of all types, styles, and media . . . all of these are useful and important in helping us learn and retain information. Why? Because there is an irrefutable fact: RUST HAPPENS!

Not only do we need a constant quest for knowledge and understanding, but we must also master the art of maintenance. If you own a car, a house, a boat, or any other possession, you understand the role of prevention and maintenance. The principles that we are trying to teach must be reevaluated and reconsidered, reexamined and reestablished on a continual basis. We need to maintain and refresh the knowledge and principles that we have embraced and come to love.

It would seem to go without saying that if we want to fill our lives with the uplifting, the moral, the Christ-like, and the charitable, we must avoid like a plague any and all forms of pornography with its carnal, sensual, and filthy sources. Whether we are talking about reading material or pictures, the Internet, chat rooms, bars, strip clubs, or videos, this information fills our precious brains, which do not vomit, regurgitate, or dispose of the filth that we take in.

Our brains are unlike our physical bodies that with rare fatal exceptions, are equipped to handle the effects of poisonous, diseased, or filthy food. The brain, however, is like a sponge that soaks up all information yet is not able to extract and dispose of that information; once we have put filth in, it can be recalled again and again.

IF I HAD MY LIFE TO LIVE OVER…

I'd dare to make more mistakes next time.
I'd relax; I'd limber up.
I would be sillier than I have been this trip.
I would take fewer things seriously.
I would take more chances.
I would climb more mountains and swim more rivers.
I would perhaps have more actual troubles,
but I'd have fewer imaginary ones.
You see, I'm one of those people who live sensibly
and sanely hour after hour, day after day.
Oh, I've had my moments, and if I had to do it over again,
I'd have more of them.
In fact, I'd try to have nothing else.
Just moments, one after another, instead of living
So many years ahead of each day.
I've been one of those persons who never goes anywhere without
a thermometer, a hot water bottle, a raincoat, and a parachute.
If I had to do it again, I would travel lighter than I have.
If I had my life to live over, I would start barefoot
earlier in the spring, and stay that way later in the fall.
I would go to more dances.
I would ride more merry-go-rounds.
I would pick more daisies.[60]

This last poem is tender insight from someone whose days remaining here in mortality are probably numbered. The author of this poem was eighty-five when she wrote it. This is good advice for those of us with a few years left to travel this Earth.

The next poem was written by author and poet Robert Louis Stevenson (1850–1894). It has become a favorite over time and has been read at the funerals and birthday celebrations of some of the most recognized celebrities and politicians throughout the world.

THAT MAN IS A SUCCESS

That man is a success who has lived well,
Laughed often and loved much;
Who has gained the respect of intelligent men

And the love of children;
Who has filled his niche and accomplished his task;
Who leaves the world better than he found it,
Whether by an improved poppy,
A perfect poem or a rescued soul;
Who never lacked appreciation of earth's beauty
or failed to express it;
Who looked for the best in others
and gave the best he had.[61]

I have in my office a mobile—one of those hanging structures with a central weight that pulls everything into balance. The weight at the bottom balances the objects (birds, airplanes, etc.) that twirl above it. I use the mobile to suggest to people that, in their own identities, they have many relationships. They have a relationship with their spouse, relationships with their children and their in-laws; they also have a relationship with God. But the most important relationship they have is with themselves.

I demonstrate this visually by pointing out the mobile. When the bottom object is likened to our relationship with ourselves, we can see that if the weight at the bottom is disturbed, all the other objects, or our other relationships, are quickly thrown out of balance, and they just flop around. Mental health is a balancing act—an act worth learning if we would experience joy in this life.

Consider the word *gestalt*, a Germanic word with no real equivalent in the English language. However, the word basically means that "the whole is greater than the sum of its parts."[62]

Let me draw a mental image for you. Imagine you have been gathering building materials. You have rafters, trusses, 2 x 4s, 2 x 8s, 2 x 10s, bricks, a pile of nails, several bags of cement, a couple of doors, insulation, several windows, shingles, wiring, lights, paint, carpet, vinyl, and even a heating and cooling system. You have a lot of materials, but do you have a building? Do these abstract items when looked at separately equal a home, an office, a church, or any other type of building? What is missing?

Of course, a master builder has to take an architectural plan or drawing, know the function of each item that has been gathered, start from the bottom up, and methodically put the pieces together until they create a foundation, floors, sheet rock walls, door frames, ceilings, wiring, electricity, duct work, plumbing, and so forth.

It is a somewhat difficult prospect to picture the finished product, especially if this is your first building, but you persist because you believe the master builder has designed a good plan, has gathered appropriate materials, and has hired qualified workers to do each part. After a given time, the foundation, framework, walls, doors, roof, electricity, and plumbing take shape, and it becomes obvious that the building is going to be a sanctuary of some type. A cathedral? A church? It's all of these—it is a home!

Because of the faith you have in the master builder, you follow the plan carefully and take pride in the workmanship and details of your home. You put the best you have into this home, and as it takes shape, you gain appreciation and respect for the different components and workers who apply their trade to the completion of this home.

Finally, the outside is completed. Then the plumbing is installed, the walls and ceilings are painted, the electricity is hooked up, the carpet and vinyl are installed, and your home is ready to move into.

Each component, each worker, each step is symbolic of the life that each of us live. You are incomplete without each experience that has shaped you. Good, bad, tragic, sad, or wonderful, each step, each experience has made us the person we are today, and each step and each experience tomorrow will make you who you can be.

Don't resent the bent nails, the itchy insulation, the sawdust, the slivers, the messy mortar, or even the tacky strips holding the carpet down, for each one of them has played a valuable part of the building you now admire with its strong walls, brick entry, locking doors, and plush carpet.

Can you say to the building at this point that you didn't need the insulation in the walls, that you didn't need the tacky strips holding the carpet in place, and you didn't need the fuse box to safely hook up the electricity? No, of course not.

In conclusion, like the completed home, you are Heavenly Father's master creation. Your experiences have molded who you are today and will further determine who you will be tomorrow. The pain, happiness, trials, successes, and failures are like the itchy insulation or the bent nails—you may have wished to not have so much or so many of them, but every piece was important. This is gestalt; this is synergism; this is the eternal scheme of things, and you are the masterpiece!

Without a doubt, self-discovery, self-mastery, self-esteem, and self-evaluation all require courage. They require taking action, changing or forming correct thought patterns, and implementing the things you learn so they become delicious to you (see Alma 32:28).

Your self-image is merely a reflection of what different people, institutions, and your own inner voice shows you. The mirror causing the reflection may be a trick, set up in the carnival of modern society to picture you as taller, fatter, dumber, or older than you really are. Gaining an accurate perception of yourself requires searching and testing. Both the history and the theology of the gospel of Jesus Christ suggest to me that only by undertaking this journey in earnest can you and I prepare ourselves for the trials to come.

When the Ten Commandments were given to Moses, I believe they were purposely made very short. But, I think these simple commandments trigger many complex emotions and ideas. In that same vein, I would like to offer a few emotional commandments:

EMOTIONAL COMMANDMENTS

1. I shall not compare myself. If it's not fair to compare children, it's certainly not any more fair to compare adults. If I am going to compare people, I should do it on a basis of several criteria and certainly not just one or two. It's not mentally healthy for me to discredit or devalue myself through false comparisons.

2. I shall remember that perfection is a process, not a status. Life is a journey, not a destination. It is a process that prepares me for something more on the other side. I believe there are no perfect people; therefore, there is always room for growth. Perfectionism may be spelled P-A-R-A-L-Y-S-I-S. I must learn to accept failure in order to have success. A good skier does not learn to be a great skier without falling down. I fail if I take off the skis and refuse to ski again. Nobody started out perfect, but to become afraid to the point that I refuse to try is the failure.

3. I shall control my actions while working on my feelings. Actions are all that can be measured and absolutely judged. It is natural to want to act on feelings (the natural man is an enemy to God), but by doing so I only compound the emotions and thereby cycle myself into wars. Curbing destructive actions prevents feelings from escalating into out-of-control situations. The feelings are thus dealt with and without war games. I have never known anyone to be convicted in court based on his thoughts. However, if I have acted on inappropriate feelings or thoughts, I can be convicted because physically or verbally I am now guilty. Everyone has private thoughts, and many of them are undesirable. But there are numerous ways to deal with them. However, harsh and critical judgments of my feelings or thoughts don't help. My thoughts don't damn me unless they become actions or I ruminate and allow those thoughts to stay. Simply having harsh, critical, or negative thoughts means nothing, except that I am human. It's what I do when those thoughts come that makes the difference.

4. I shall not let guilt serve neurotic purposes. I should remember that I have a critical parent inside of me who interacts with my hurt, fearful, adaptive child (also inside of me) in such a way that the fearful, adaptive child plays a game of victimization. In that game, I refuse to let the guilt go. I become so shame-based that the grace and love of the Atonement are rejected. I will be aware of these signs and refuse to play this game.

5. I shall not use the past to punish myself. Many scriptural references relate to the essence of repentance as a way of putting things behind me, and of no longer wallowing in my imperfections. As the woman taken in adultery was taught by the Savior, "neither do I condemn thee: go, and sin no more" (John 8:11).

6. I shall no longer think just in absolutes. That is, I will not think only in black and white, all or nothing, right or wrong. I will use appropriate words to define my actual situation. I will not see just two options; I will define people and experiences according to a wide range of alternatives.

7. I shall realize the difference between feeling bad and feeling guilty. I realize that I feel bad about many things, and these feelings are probably appropriate. But guilt implies that I did something wrong to promote the situation. I will remember that some people try to encumber others with their own guilt. I will shun guilt that does not belong to me. If I had no control, I would have no responsibility and therefore no guilt.

8. I shall give others their agency. We fought a great war in heaven over whether people should have the freedom to choose. I won't like some of the choices people make, but I will let them choose anyway. I have the responsibility to encourage, admonish, and teach correct principles, but other people have the freedom and the obligation to choose for themselves.

9. I shall remember reality testing. I will remember to consider other explanations and not make quick assumptions about what is going on in the world. I shall remember that it's easy to observe a situation but more difficult to interpret it accurately.

10. I shall ultimately learn to live out of my own model of respect. Too many people are too busy trying to please everyone else by trying to be what others want them to be. It's good to have role models and to accept encouragement, but if I am merely a chameleon, I will end up unhappy and depressed. I cannot, ultimately, make everyone happy. Any decision I make may cause someone to question my judgment. This can be called the "one-third, one-third, one-third principle." For any decision a person makes, one-third of a given public will be happy, one-third will be critical, and one-third won't care. If I change my decisions, I only change populations.

11. I shall not define myself negatively. Too many people discredit and devalue themselves. I need to realize that I do have exceptionality and rarity that corresponds to my unique mission and responsibilities here on this earth. I will be especially careful not to discount myself out of some false understanding of morality or ethics, damning myself because I should be living a higher law.

12. I shall not deal with life and death equivalencies. I will realize that there is a major difference in wanting something and in seeing it as an absolute necessity. I will define for myself my wants verses my needs.

13. I shall not double-bind myself or others. Imagine how terrifying it may be to the brain to hear words or phrases like, "I can't stand it," "I need," or "I must have." Too many times people set up a system in which nobody can win. To determine whether I'm in a double bind, I will ask myself if the circumstances were radically changed, would I still be unhappy? (For instance, do I want my husband to help me around the house, but I am double bound because this makes me feel in some way inadequate? It takes a lot of maturity to understand double binding and to be honest with myself about these problems.)

14. I shall not have to have absolute guarantees in life. I know life would be a lot easier if I had guarantees, but what if I never did anything without one? When I buy a new car, I'll get the guarantee. But, for most other things, I realize that caution and good judgment are probably all I have working for me.

15. I shall not compare my reality to a fantasy. Fantasies are perfect and reality just cannot compete with them. I will not compare my spouse or children with the unrealistic portrayals in magazine photos and romance novels.

16. I shall want what I have. This is a cheerful commandment but not nearly as simple as it sounds. I do not necessarily have to be totally satisfied with what I have, but I will feel that I want what I have. I am truly invested in it, and I want to improve upon it. This does not mean that I cannot work for something better.

17. I shall live with probability, not possibility. The Savior told us not to worry but to be as free as the lilies of the field (see Matthew 6:28–31). Many fears are clearly unrealistic; people often worry about possibilities instead of probabilities. "Could this happen?" "What if this were going on?" "Do you think this is possible?" These questions initiate unnecessary anxiety. Psychologists often testify in court, and lawyers, trying to prove their cases, love to couch things in the framework of probabilities because if they can demonstrate a possibility of innocence—a shadow of a doubt—they win their case. The prosecution's case must be airtight, because a conviction can result in taking an individual's property, his freedom, or even his life. But what kinds of possibilities should we be concerned about in our everyday lives? As you read this book right now, could a meteorite come crashing through your roof and wipe you out? Possibly, but you needn't reasonably worry about it because the probability is incredibly remote. Nevertheless, some people worry themselves sick about all sorts of possibilities, from their health or their work to financial disasters and wars. They often find themselves so reactive and panicky that they become agoraphobic—that is, they simply avoid all situations they fear.

With regard to this last commandment, I hope and pray that those of us blessed enough to have families, friends, employment, church families, and the necessities of life will prioritize the most important to the least important things in our lives and try to keep them in order.

I love the following poem as it describes taking the road that others resist, the road to change, to health, to peace, and to happiness.

THE ROAD NOT TAKEN

Two roads diverged in a yellow wood
And sorry I could not travel both
And be one traveler, long I stood
 And looked down one as far as I could
To where it bent in the undergrowth;
Then took the other, as just as fair

And having perhaps the better claim,
Because it was grassy and wanted wear;
Though as for that the passing there
Had worn them really about the same.

And both that morning equally lay
In leaves no step had trodden black
Oh, I kept the first for another day!
Yet knowing how way leads on to way,
I doubted if I should ever come back.

I shall be telling this with a sigh
Somewhere ages and ages hence:
Two roads diverged in a wood, and I—
I took the one less traveled by,
And that has made all the difference.[63]

Congratulations! Continue to move forward, to pursue, to fail, to pick yourself back up, to dream, to work, and to pray! And remember: the joy is in the journey!

ENDNOTES

1. Socrates. Online. "Quotations by Author," *Quoteland.com.* Accessed 2006; available from www.quoteland.com/author. asp?author_Id=137.
2. Nicholson, John. "Come, Follow Me," *Hymns of The Church of Jesus Christ of Latter-day Saints.* Salt Lake City: The Church of Jesus Christ of Latter-day Saints, 1985.
3. Berra, Yogi. Online. "Yogi Berra Quotes," *Digitaldreemdoor.com.* Accessed 2006; available from www.digitaldreamdoor.com/pages/ quotes/yogiberra.html.
4. Steve Young story as related by Jeanine Buckingham.
5. Steve Young story as related by Jeanine Buckingham.
6. Sisyphus. Online. Available from www.cloudnet.com/edrbsass/sisy-phus.htm.
7. Peterson, Lyle R. "Self-Mastery."
8. LDS Art by Intermountain
9. Malone, Walter. Online. "Opportunity," *On the Damascus Road.* Accessed 2006; available from www.netten.net/~kenn/poemwm10. htm.

10. Anonymous. Online. "Pain Stayed So Long," *Pain Research Institute*. Accessed 2006; available from www.healpain.net/articles/helpain.html.

11. Stevenson, Mary. "Footprints."

12. Stewart, John, ed. *The Concise Oxford Dictionary of Proverbs*. Oxford University Press, 1998.

13. Heinlein, Robert Anson. Online. *Time Enough For Love*. Available from www.pkshiu.com/pk/q/q-71.html and http://users.innevi.com/~thor/wisdom.htm.

14. *Webster's New Collegiate Dictionary, 2nd Edition*.

15. "Biography of Helen Keller," Online. *Helen Keller Services for the Blind*. Accessed 2006; available from www.helenkeller.org/graphicversion/bio.html.

16. Smithee, Tracey. "Poignant Thought."

17. *Webster's New Collegiate Dictionary, 2nd Edition*.

18. Lee, Harold B. *Stand Ye In Holy Places: Selected Sermons and Writings of President Harold B. Lee*. Salt Lake City: Deseret Book, 1974, 186.

19. Miller, Evelyn. 1998 Christmas newsletter.

20. "Orestes Mythology" Online. *Wikipedia*. Accessed 2006; available from en.wikipedia.org/wiki/orestes.

21. Author Unknown.

22. Niebuhr, Karl Paul Reinhold. Online. "Serenity Prayer," *An Illustrated Alcoholic Anonymous Bibliography*. Accessed 2006; available from www.aabibliography.com/neibuhr.html.

23. Marshall, Thurgood. Online. "Thurgood Marshall Quotes," *Thinkexist.com*. Accessed 2006; available from thinkexist.com/quotes/thurgood_marshall/.

24. Kimball, Edward and Andrew Kimball. *Biography of Spencer W. Kimball*. Salt Lake City: Bookcraft, 1978, 265, 303, 395-427.

25. Einstein, Albert. Online. "Albert Einstein Quotes," *Brainy Quote*. Accessed 2006; available from brainyquote.com/quotes/quotes/a/alberteins121993.htm.

26. Le Joly, Edward. *Mother Teresa of Calcutta: A Biography*. San Francisco: Harper & Row, 1985, 321.

27. Author Unknown. *Autobiography in Five Short Chapters*.

28. Author Unknown. Inspired by Mahatma Ghandi.

29. John L. Lund, "The Myth We Call Perfection," CD. American Fork: Covenant Communications, 2003.

30. Author Unknown. Online. "A Parent's Love Poem," *Luv's Creations.* Accessed 2006; available from www.luvscreations.com/poems/love/parentsluv.htm.

31. "Memorandum From a Child" *The Message International.* New York: June 1991, reprint, 40.

32. Jefferson, Thomas. Online. *The Quotations Page.* Accessed 2006; available from www.quotationspage.com/quote/27616.html.

33. McKay, David O. Online. "David McKay Quotes," *Thinkexist.com.* Accessed 2006; available from en.thinkexist.com/quotes/david_mckay/.

34. Hall, Steven J.

35. Holland, Jeffrey R. Online. "Of Souls, Symbols, and Sacraments," *Speeches.* Accessed 2006; available from www.speeches.byu.edu.

36. Watson, Wendy. Online. "Personal Purity and Intimacy," *Speeches.* Accessed 2006; available from www.speeches.byu.edu

37. Author Unknown. "'Twas a Sheep." Available from www.geocities.com/Hollywood/Hills/9609/poetryjs.html and http://www.sunshin.org/treasure4.htm.

38. Czerny, Peter G. "Excess Express," *LDSfilm.com.* Accessed 2006; available from www.ldsfilm.com/bio/bioC3.html.

39. *Webster's New Collegiate Dictionary, 2nd Edition.*

40. Einstein, Albert. Online. "Collected Quotes from Albert Einstein." Accessed 2006; available from rescomp.stanford.edu/~cheshire/EinsteinQuotes.html.

41. Einstein, Albert. Online. "Albert Einstein Quotes," *Brainy Quote.* Accessed 2006; available from www.brainyquote.com/quotes/quotes/a/alberteins129798.html.

42. Robinson, Edwin Arlington. Online. "Richard Cory" Available from www.ckk.chalmers.sp/fuitar/richard.cory.1yr.html.

43. Franklin, Benjamin. Online. "The Quotable Franklin" *The Electronic Ben Franklin.* Accessed 2006; available from www.ushistory.org/franklin/quotable.

44. Burroughs, John. Online. *Amicita.* Accessed 2006; available from amicitia.xanthra.com/posts/235/.

45. Williamson, Marianne. *A Return to Love: Reflections on the*

Principles of A Course in Miracles. Chapter 7, Section 3. Harper Collins, 1992.

46. Welch, Myra Brooks. Online. "Touch of the Master's Hand," *Shy's Favorite Quotes, etc.* Accessed 2006; available from www.fament. com/eric/touch.htm.

47. Kushner, Harold S. *When Bad Things Happen to Good People.*

48. TDY definition found at Perdiem.com.

49. Fulghum, Robert. *All I Really Needed To Know, I Learned In Kindergarten.* Ballantine Books, 2003.

50. Author Unknown.

51. Nelson, Zane P. *Two General Ways to Forget.*

52. McKay, David O. Online. "David McKay Quotes," *Thinkexist.com.* Accessed 2006; available from http://en.thinkexist.com/quotes/ david_mckay/

53. Nelson, Zane P. Personal History.

54. Smithee, Tracey. "Seeing Inside the Clown."

55. Frankel, Valerie. "The Accidental Virgin," *Couples Magazine.* Sept. 2002.

56. Author Unknown. Online. "After a While," *Divorce Recovery Site.* Accessed 2006; available from home.att.net/~velvet-hammer/comesthedawn.html .

57. Einstein, Albert. Online. *Experience.* Accessed 2006; available from www.kibbe.com/experience.html.

58. Pavlov, Ivan Petrovich. Online. *Ivan Pavlov.* Accessed 2006; available from evolution.massey.ac.nz/assign2/KD/finalpavlov.html.

59. "Indian Boy and the Snake." Online. Available from http://www. scoutxingcom/scoutmaster/scmin165.htm.

60. Stair, Nadine. "If I Had My Life to Live Over Again."

61. Stevenson, Robert Louis. Online. "That Man Is A Success." Available from www.edinburghacademy.org.uk/seniorprospectur/ alumni.htm.

62. *Word Reference.com English Dictionary.* Online. Accessed 2006; available from www.wordreference.com/definition/gestalt

63. Frost, Robert. Online. "The Road Not Taken," *Classic Poetry Pages.* Accessed 2006; available from poetrypages.lemon8.nl/life/roadnottaken/roadnottaken.htm.

ABOUT THE AUTHOR

Dr. Zane Nelson is a licensed psychologist who has a private practice in Boise, Idaho. His clinical practice extends to outpatient and inpatient services.

He received his Ph.D. from Brigham Young University and a postdoctoral certificate from The Johns Hopkins University in psychiatry and behavioral sciences (suicidology). As a suicidologist he has published articles on suicide, worked as a medical examiner and/or a consultant for coroner's offices. Dr. Nelson brings to his writings a wide range of experiences in crisis intervention, substance abuse, and clinical evaluations (chief of the Bureau of Substance Abuse—Idaho; ran Narcotics Rehabilitation Act program, prescription dependency programs, 24-hour crisis services).

Dr. Nelson has published several Journal articles and chapters as well as a book Sanity Strategies for Everyday Mormons. He has held numerous Church callings including the office of bishop and has served in several bishoprics and high councils. He and his wife, Terry, have had six children.